THE CUT FLOWER

HANDBOOK

SELECT, PLANT, GROW, AND HARVEST GORGEOUS BLOOMS

LISA MASON ZIEGLER

OF THE GARDENER'S WORKSHOP

WITH CONTRIBUTIONS BY JESSICA GRAVEN

COOL SPRINGS PRESS

Quarto.com

First Published in 2023 by Cool Springs Press, an imprint of
The Quarto Group, 100 Cummings Center, Suite 265-D,
Beverly, MA 01915, USA.
T (978) 282-9590 F (978) 283-2742

Cool Springs Press titles are also available at discount
for retail, wholesale, promotional, and bulk purchase. For
details, contact the Special Sales Manager by email at
specialsales@quarto.com or by mail at The Quarto Group,
Attn: Special Sales Manager, 100 Cummings Center, Suite
265-D, Beverly, MA 01915, USA.

28 27 26 25 24   1 2 3 4 5

ISBN: 978-0-7603-8210-3

Digital edition published in 2024
eISBN: 978-0-7603-8213-4

Library of Congress Cataloging-in-Publication
Data is available.

Design and page layout: Kelley Galbreath
Front cover images: Robert W. Schamerhorn
Back cover images: Robert W. Schamerhorn (top left
  and bottom right) and The Gardener's Workshop
  (right column, top and center)
Photography: Robert W. Schamerhorn, except pages 3, 4
  (top middle), 5 (middle, bottom), 6–7, 26, 37, 64, 65 (all
  except right), 66, 68, 71, 73, 74, 76–77, 78 (top), 83, 85
  (bottom), 86, 88, 91, 94, 98, 100, 103, 104, 106, 109, 110
  (right), 113, 116, 118 (left), 122 (left), 124, 126, 130 (top),
  133, 135, 136, 139, 141, 145, 149, 150, 153 (bottom left,
  bottom right), 154, 158, 159 (top), 161, 163, 164, 166, 170,
  185, 189 (top), 217 (top) The Gardener's Workshop; page
  9 Luke & Ashley Photography; and page 127 Thomas
  McCurdy, Ardelia Farm
Illustration: Preston Montague

Printed in China

To the grandmas
that shared their love
of gardening.

―――――――――――

Grandma, your peonies still
bloom each spring. You'd love them.
Thank you.

Contents

FAR LEFT *Line of Zinnia 'Benary's Giants';* **LEFT TOP** *Sweet William 'Super Duplex'; Sunflower 'Lemonade';* **LEFT, MIDDLE** *Celosia 'Sylphid', 'Sunday', 'Hi-Z', 'Cramer's Amazon', and 'Flamingo Feather'; Bachelor Buttons 'Boy' and 'Classic';* **LEFT, BOTTOM** *Cockscomb 'Asuka'; Iceland Poppy 'Champagne Bubbles'*

Introduction

Two Gardeners Became One Flower Farmer

I was a new gardener when I learned about cutting gardens. I stumbled on an article in a magazine while I sat in the waiting room of my grandma's nursing home, and it lit me on fire and changed the course of my life. It said you could grow cut flowers in a backyard and even sell them as a business. I couldn't stop thinking about growing flowers. It felt like I had found my calling, but at the same time, it seemed totally out of my reach.

As the story goes, my gardening love story was meant to be. During the 1990s when I stumbled upon that article, I had just married Steve, who had a heart of gold. Steve was a gardener, and he came with a wonderful gardening dowry. In fact, his sweet bungalow home surrounded by drifts of hydrangeas and a large vegetable patch is part of what led me to ask him out for a date.

On my first visit to Steve's home for a lunch date, he served fresh string beans from his garden and a pound cake he had baked. After lunch, we took

a walk around his yard, and he shared the rich history of his family's gardens and those that had come before him. Little did Steve and I know what was taking root that day. Steve and I married in 1996, the year following the lunch that started it all.

Soon after marrying, I took over the day-to-day chores of the vegetable gardens alongside Steve. Slowly, I began inching cut flowers into the vegetable patch, starting with a row of zinnias that I cut each week to take to my grandma. Successful in growing and harvesting those zinnias as well as other cut flowers I added with Steve's encouragement, I launched Ziegler Garden in 1998 as the start of my cut-flower-growing business.

Lemons into Lemonade

My little city flower-farming business blossomed and grew. At first, I struggled because of my lack of "acreage" and the residential setting I found myself in that prevented having a greenhouse. In cut-flower-growing circles, it was understood that having structures and acreage was a requirement for success. Since these were not an option for me, I pushed on, honed my gardening skills, and found a way.

I learned to garden intensely, maximizing abundance in my small space, and to grow top-quality flowers outdoors in the elements. After learning

FROM FAR LEFT
A big part of my flower farming success story is because of Steve's support and willingness to help with any job.

Making a bed in a cool-season hardy annual garden in my early years. This 8hp Troybilt tiller was a part of that "garden dowry" that came with Steve and that I still use today.

about the soil-blocking seed-starting method, I was able to produce the volume of transplants needed to supply my three-season gardens. The space savviness of this method allowed me to grow thousands of seedlings indoors on shelving in limited space using grow lights.

In the early days, my half-acre (0.2 ha) working cutting garden produced thousands of flower stems each week in season. At first, I sold to one high-volume florist only, but as more flowers came, I added more florists and became a supplier for Colonial Williamsburg in Williamsburg, Virginia. I started selling at farmers' markets, created my bouquet drop-off subscription and members-only flower market programs, and sold to grocery store chains. Learning to grow abundant, top-quality blooms with my limited indoor and outdoor spaces made lemonade out of what had once seemed like lemons.

Another piece of what made our gardens so special was our neighbor's forty-acre (16 ha) horse-boarding farm. Being surrounded by green pastures and horses grazing made our place an oasis in the midst of the city. In 2010, when the opportunity came to purchase the acre and a half (0.6 ha) adjoining our farm, it led my flower farm straight into the "high-production years." That half-acre (0.2 ha) working cutting garden grew to one and a half acres (0.6 ha) that produced ten to fifteen thousand stems of flowers each week in season. We were starting more than one hundred thousand seedlings throughout each year and selling close to a quarter million stems of flowers each season!

An Unexpected Twist

An unexpected twist came as my business developed beyond growing and selling cut flowers: I started teaching others how to do it. At first, I was helping home gardeners learn how to grow and cut flowers, but then I started teaching wannabe flower farmers to do as I was doing. During this time, I found that my strongest gifts are teaching and encouraging others, particularly those who think they can't do it or that it is out of their reach—just like I had.

As my speaking went national, students began requesting access to the same gardening tools, supplies, and seeds I used and spoke about in my programs. In 2005, I started The Gardener's Workshop (TGW), my online garden store and educational platform. TGW grew as I traveled the country teaching others how to grow cut flowers. In 2014, my first book, *Cool Flowers* was published, followed by *Vegetables Love Flowers* in 2018. During this time, I launched a library of online courses on flower farming and home gardening to reach students worldwide. The TGW online educational platform includes resources such as my *Field & Garden* podcast and blog and video how-to guides.

TheGardenersWorkshop.com has grown from a little urban flower farm into a company of like-minded gardeners and farmers that have made it their mission to help equip others to grow cut flowers on any scale. Here is The Gardener's Workshop crew under our saucer magnolia.

Today, as a 100 percent field and garden grower, I am thankful I was pushed to learn how to manage outdoor growing for a crop that is often thought to require indoor growing. Growing outdoors in giant gardens has kept my teaching relevant and in touch with home gardeners along with providing opportunities for beginning and seasoned flower farmers.

I was enticed to write *The Cut Flower Handbook* to provide my simple growing and harvesting practices as well as flower selections. In this book, I share the enjoyment that growing cut flowers can bring into your backyard, whether for personal pleasure or for market. And though there are differences between a for-pleasure and a for-profit cutting garden, the journey to grow the flowers starts in the same place.

After more than two decades of growing, selling, teaching, and sharing about the simplicity of growing cut flowers, I couldn't be more thankful for that day, sitting with my grandma. Had I not been there, I would not be here.

one

The Cut Flower Concept

I FELL HEAD-OVER-HEELS IN LOVE with the process and life of a cutting garden.

If you love flowers and gardening, too, this garden allows, encourages, and even needs you to exercise your favorite gardening muscles and offers spectacular results. On these pages, I share the surprising gardening lessons I learned while going from a home gardener to a cut-flower farmer that, I hope, will help you grow fistfuls of flowers for your pleasure—because who knows where it may lead.

Early in my flower-farming career, I learned that annual plants produced the most stems of flowers over the longest period of time, and that they would be a great fit for my small-space urban farm. Including both warm- and cool-season annual plants as my primary crops, along with treating the garden as a cutting garden, taught me some surprising gardening lessons. This garden's recommended small size produces abundance; its care is simpler than imagined and the rewards of the flowers are beyond expectations. Setting up the garden as outlined on these pages, and committing a small amount of time each week to tend it, will bring the best surprise of all: a garden full of blooms that just keep on coming.

The size of the cutting garden has a direct impact on success or failure. The tendency is to think a large garden is needed to produce enough flowers for the need or want. But the truth is, when it comes to a cutting garden, **smaller is better.** Going small and following the practices of a cutting garden will provide more cut flowers from a smaller space for a longer period of time. Going bigger often leads to skipping harvests because there are more flowers than needed—and so begins the garden's spiral of decline. Skipping harvests is the beginning of the end of a cutting garden's life. Go small (see page 36 for garden size recommendations).

Here I am, harvesting cosmos in the early summer garden; flower beds left to right: gomphrena, cosmos, and hibiscus.

The care of this garden is streamlined when it is set up as a working garden instead of treating it as part of a landscape. When I ventured away from being a home gardener and into flower-farming circles, I learned so many eye-opening gardening practices, including how much closer together plants in a cutting garden are planted because they are continually harvested—it's like they undergo heavy weekly pruning. Following this one simple technique not only produced more flowers but also produced taller, straighter stems and it helped the flowers' growth outcompete the potential weed growth in the bed. These types of practices made it so much smoother for me to find my way to becoming a successful cut-flower grower.

Throughout this book, I share flower farming insider tips to make the reality and upkeep of a cutting garden simpler whether you are a home gardener or a flower farmer. In this section, you'll find my guiding principles for a successful cutting garden.

June is when the cool and warm season annuals overlap and are in abundance. Bobo, veteran flower arranger and TGW crew member, filled Grandpa Ziegler's toolbox with sunflowers, zinnias, mint, yarrow, sweet peas, poppy pods, godetia, scabiosa, craspedia, feverfew, and strawflowers.

The Three-Season Annual Cutting Garden

Growing both cool- and warm-season annual plants allows the continual reuse of the same garden space with a diverse selection of flowers to harvest. As the garden changes with the seasons, the widest selection of flowers, and colors, can be planted in a given space. This garden lets you grow the pastels of spring followed by the bright colors of summer, and closes with the cozy colors of fall as the harvest season comes to an end.

The flowers featured in this book are broken into warm and cool sections for easy planning. Cool-season hardy annuals, such as sweet peas, poppies, and snapdragons, perform best and prefer cool to cold conditions, whereas warm-season tender annuals, such as zinnias, sunflowers, and basil, thrive in warm to hot conditions. Planting each respective group in their preferred conditions leads to plants that thrive naturally with fewer inputs from the gardener. These plants produce more abundantly with longer stems, and they prove to be more disease- and pest-resistant. Doing a little homework to determine when to plant each of these groups of annual flowers in your seasonal conditions, and sticking with that timing, will change your gardening experience.

Is It a Warm-Season Tender Annual or a Cool-Season Hardy Annual?

Deciding when to plant a specific annual in the garden begins with determining what type of annual it is. The confusion over this simple question has led many to forgo growing some of the most beautiful annual flowers for fear of repeating past failures due to incorrect planting times. Gaining an understanding of the two types of annuals and their very different needs will help you bring them into your garden. To get the planting time right start with this question: Is it a warm- or cool-season annual?

Why are we so confused? Because the term "annual plant" is often used in a general manner to identify the most widely recognized group of annuals, the warm-season tender annuals. This implies that there is just one type of annual, which is not the case. Furthermore, the fact that the cool-season hardy annual lifecycle can span more than one growing season fuels confusion because of the similarities to a biennial plant's lifecycle completed over two years' time.

Because this information is often omitted on seed packets, I put on my detective's hat to learn whether a flower new to me is a cool- or warm-season annual. I look for hints in the description like "sow in spring as soon as the soil can be worked." This type of phrase flags for me that it might be a cool-season annual. If no further information is available, I go with my hunch and trial plant it to see what happens. Finding the proper annual family identification gets easier with practice and is the key to planting at the proper time.

Why Succession Planting?

To make the three-season garden even more productive and diverse, consider extending the bloom times. You can do this by planting flowers more than once during your longest growing season. For example, my longest growing season is summer, with temperatures averaging 70 to 90°F (21 to 32°C)

There are two types of annual plants in this book:

1 Cool-season hardy annuals
2 Warm-season tender annuals

Both complete their similar lifecycle within one year, but each is planted into very different conditions and according to different timelines.

WHAT TYPE OF ANNUAL IS IT?

- Start by entering into a search engine: "What type of annual is [plant name]?"
- I recommend using reliable search results from universities and botanical gardens.
- Once you know the type, write it on the seed packet to help you learn and not rely on memory.

flower farmer insider tip

Store seed packets grouped by type of annual. Keep all cool-season seeds together in a container and warm-season seeds in a separate container. When the time comes for cool-season seed starting, bring out that container, and all your choices will be there.

for 200 days. I can plant warm-season tender annuals several times each summer to extend the quality and quantity of blooms produced. This practice is known as *succession planting*.

Another discovery I made on this cut-flower journey is that succession planting makes gardening more manageable and can even nudge us toward becoming better gardeners. It feeds our strongest urges as gardeners. Tasks like seed starting, bed preparation, planting, mulching, and other chores can be done throughout the seasons, in smaller pieces, in place of a mad dash in spring in an attempt to get it all done at once. Practicing succession planting encourages pacing ourselves to spread out the chores and the harvest over time, which leads to gardening success.

Succession planting allows us to set aside that feeling of "I'm late or behind." It encourages picking up and getting started with the appropriate tasks for that place in your succession-planting timeline. It is liberating and makes gardening manageable. I am often asked, "Is it too late to do this or plant that?" My answer is universal, "Yes, it is too late for *that*, but it is the right time to do *this*." There is almost always something to do in or for the succession-planted garden; we don't need to catch up if we focus on the chores of that moment in time and go forward.

The most challenging step in succession planting is removing the declining plantings in a timely manner. Recognizing when it is time to remove a planting from the garden may not be difficult, but having the willpower to do it can be. This gets easier once you experience the results. To practice growing a three-season cutting garden, whether a small bed or an acre, you must remember that, to keep this garden producing and as weed-free as possible, plantings should be pulled once they begin to decline to make way for the next planting. When you find yourself looking for a "good one to cut and keep," it is time to remove the planting. Resisting this step has results similar to that of skipping harvests—before long, there aren't clean flowers to harvest. The garden and your interest decline.

Succession planting is at the root of the home gardener finding a way to fit gardening in among life's demands. It makes it possible for successful farmers to produce an ongoing supply of quality blooms and create manageable workflows. I have become a better gardener. I am no longer pulled to jump ahead and plant warm-season tender annuals into cool conditions, earlier than recommended, because now, in late winter, I am busy with cool-season hardy annual seeds to start, and my fall-planted plants are coming to life in the garden. I even find myself, during the cold, short days of winter, venturing out to investigate what is happening in the garden. Succession planting expands and enriches gardening and brings the shoulder seasons of early spring, fall, and even winter to life.

Planting Warm and Cool Annuals

Giving plants a great start is a lesson I learned the hard way, planting hundreds of thousands of transplants throughout my career and living with both the successes and failures that were a result of my planting timing. Farmers have a unique perspective on growing plants because of the volume of plants they grow. The volume makes it easy to see and evaluate the wins and the losses. This journey gave me a front-row seat to experience how abundant and carefree plants can be when they thrive, as well as the problems they can have when they struggle. The timing of when we plant is key to less care and more long-term success.

Planting into the seasonal weather conditions that a seed or transplant needs allows them to immediately begin growing in the garden. When planting seeds in the garden, this means they sprout more quickly, which helps the plant outcompete the weed seeds. Transplants immediately begin growing roots to become established faster. Plants getting off to this type of start usually bloom earlier, produce taller stems and more of them, require less care, and are more disease and pest resistant. It may sound silly, but a seed or plant that gets busy immediately when planted leads to a happier healthy plant life.

Planting outside the recommended seasonal weather conditions can result in seeds and transplants that are shocked and stressed, which delays the sprouting and growing process. My experience has been that, when I plant earlier or later than recommended, the plants often survive, but they seldom go on to thrive to become healthy producers. Seeds and plants that sit in the garden waiting for their preferred conditions can get into all kinds of trouble, like waterlogging, pests, and diseases, which are then commonly blamed for the failure when it was likely the wrong seasonal conditions that encouraged and invited the problems to start.

Find Your Planting Windows

It is fairly straightforward to find out when you should plant warm-season tender annual plants in your garden. However, it may take a little more investigation to learn your options for planting cool-season hardy annual plants. Learning the "sweet spot" planting times for warm- and cool-season annuals will serve you well for the rest of your gardening journey. You may

This spread and the one that follows show a sample succession planting plan in the same two growing beds over the course of two full years. You'll see both cool- and warm-season annuals in various cycles of their growth at different times of the year. Year 1 flows into Year 2 with cool-season plants that overwinter.

Spring

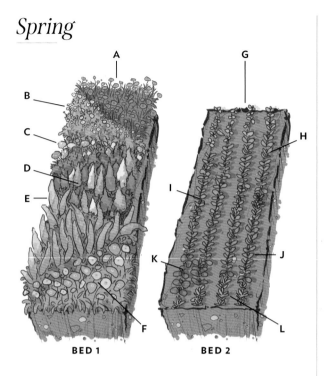

BED 1 BED 2

Summer

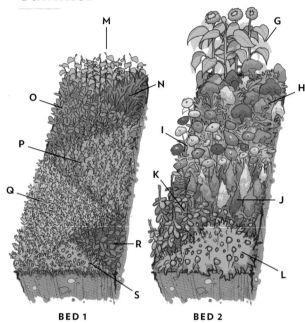

BED 1 BED 2

Bed 1

Fall planted cool-season annuals blooming in spring

A Bachelor buttons
B Feverfew
C Sweet William
D Snapdragons
E Bells of Ireland
F Poppies

Bed 2

Warm-season annual seedlings planted in spring

G Sunflowers
H Celosia (cockscomb type)
I Zinnia
J Celosia (plume type)
K Basil
L Gomphrena

Bed 1

Second summer planting of warm-season annual transplants

M Sunflowers
N Grasses
O Zinnia
P Cosmos
Q Marigold
R Basil
S Gomphrena

Bed 2

Spring planted warm-season annuals now in bloom

G Sunflowers
H Celosia (cockscomb type)
I Zinnia
J Celosia (plume type)
K Basil
L Gomphrena

Fall

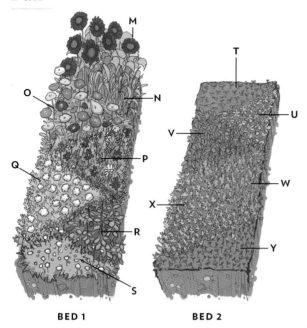

BED 1   **BED 2**

Bed 1

Second warm season annual
planting blooming in fall

M Sunflowers
N Grasses
O Zinnia
P Cosmos
Q Marigold
R Basil
S Gomphrena

Bed 2

Fall planting of cool-season annuals
that will winter over in the garden

T Larkspur
U Monarda
V Snapdragons
W Statice
X Orlaya
Y Chinese forget-me-nots

Winter

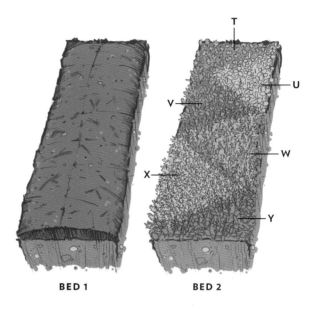

BED 1   **BED 2**

Bed 1

Bed put to fallow for winter
Cover soil with mulch or cover crop for winter

Bed 2

Young cool-season seedlings ready to
overwinter

T Larkspur
U Monarda
V Snapdragons
W Statice
X Orlaya
Y Chinese forget-me-nots

Continue to Year 2 ➥

Spring

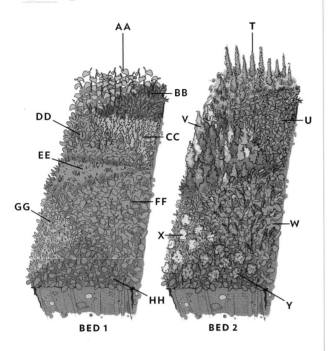

BED 1 BED 2

Summer

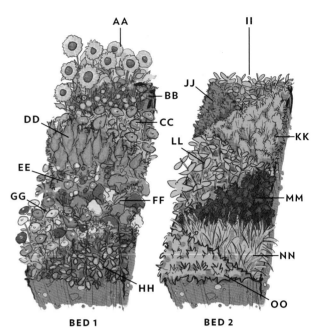

BED 1 BED 2

Bed 1

Warm-season annual seedlings planted in spring

AA Sunflowers
BB Hairy Balls
CC Zinnia
DD Celosia (plume type)
EE Sweet William
FF Celosia (cockscomb type)
GG Strawflower
HH Basil

Bed 2

Fall planted cool-season annuals blooming in spring

T Larkspur
U Monarda
V Snapdragons
W Statice
X Orlaya
Y Chinese forget-me-nots

Bed 1

Spring planted warm-season annuals now in bloom

AA Sunflowers
BB Hairy Balls
CC Zinnia
DD Celosia (plume type)
EE Sweet William
FF Celosia (cockscomb type)
GG Strawflower
HH Basil

Bed 2

Second summer planting of warm-season annual transplants

II Amaranth
JJ Marigolds
KK Cosmos
LL Zinnias
MM Hibiscus
NN Grasses
OO Marigolds

Fall

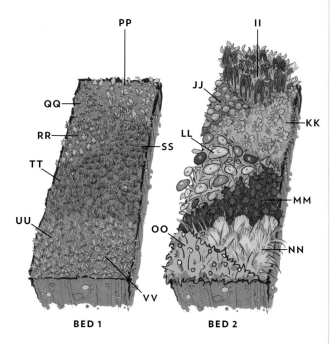

BED 1

BED 2

Bed 1

Fall planting of cool-season annuals that will winter over in the garden

PP Poppy
QQ Scabiosa
RR Dill
SS Rudbeckia
TT Craspedia
UU Calendula
VV Nigella

Bed 2

Second warm-season annual planting blooming in fall

II Amaranth
JJ Marigolds
KK Cosmos
LL Zinnias
MM Hibiscus
NN Grasses
OO Marigolds

Winter

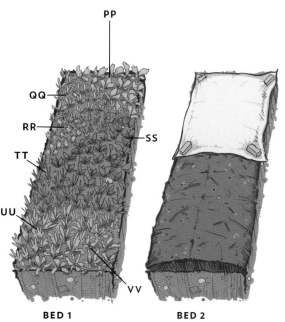

BED 1

BED 2

Bed 1

Young cool-season seedlings ready to overwinter

PP Poppy
QQ Scabiosa
RR Dill
SS Rudbeckia
TT Craspedia
UU Calendula
VV Nigella

Bed 2

Bed put to fallow for winter
Cover soil with mulch or a silage tarp for winter

Use this information to plan seed-starting and planting dates.

My garden's average dates:

First expected fall frost date: _____

Last expected spring frost date: _____

Winter lowest temperature: _____

adjust each season as you gain experience, the weather patterns change, and new flowers are added to your garden, but this information will determine your basic planting windows.

The information required to determine when you plant begins with the historic average first fall and last spring frost dates for your area, plus your average lowest winter temperatures. This information is usually available on the internet. Enter the question, "When is the first frost for [your location]?"

and so on. Other good sources of information are local gardening organizations, nurseries, and farmers. Keep in mind, when seeking average dates and temperatures, this is historical information gathered over decades, but it can help you find a starting point for your garden. Don't get overly concerned with conflicting information—just find an average and work from there.

Warm-Season Tender Annuals

Warm-season tender annuals thrive when planted and grown in warm to hot conditions. Begin planting transplants outdoors in the garden once the last expected frost date has passed, the soil has begun to warm, and we are heading into summerlike conditions. The weather signal I wait for to begin transplanting outdoors is the moment when nighttime air temperatures reach 60°F (15.5°C) or above with soil temperature at a minimum of 60°F (15.5°C).

For seeds to sprout outdoors in the garden, even warmer conditions are required. To plant seeds outdoors, wait until nighttime air temperatures are at 70°F (21°C) or above with soil temperature at a minimum of 65°F (18°C).

Having an abundance of flowers makes bouquet building something that can happen at family events like bridal showers. It's easy for guests to pick up stems and build when the flowers are stripped, ready, and waiting. Everyone leaves inspired and impressed!

The warmer the soil and air temperatures, the quicker this plant family begins its growing cycle.

Consider planting warm-season plants more than once during the season. If summer is your longest growing season, consider planting more than once for branching and single-stemmed annuals. This can extend the bloom season, increase the quality and volume of blooms, and even provide flowers in the event of storm damage or a pest issue in another location in the garden. A good example of extending the bloom season is planting single-stemmed sunflowers on a regular basis to have sunflowers all season. I start sunflower seeds each week, beginning 3 weeks before my last expected spring frost and for the following 26 weeks to have blooming sunflowers each week for my flower-farming business (see the sunflower feature, page 202, for details).

A similar process with fewer plantings can be applied to branching and single-stemmed annuals to increase blooming over a period of time (see diagram, page 16–19, for examples of multiple warm-season plantings going through the seasons).

FAR LEFT *A garden of succession planted single stem sunflowers. Because the three-week-old transplants are already a third of the way through their sixty-day lifecycle when planted, I do not use mulch, irrigation, or flower support.*

Determine whether you can plant additional warm-season plantings:

**Branching Annual Flowers
(multiple stems per plant)**

- Note the number of days until your first expected fall frost.

- Know the number of days required for that specific flower variety to grow from seed to bloom.

- To allow for harvest and growth slowdowns, like cool temperatures or fall's short days, add 30 additional days.

- Add the seed-to-bloom days to the additional 30 days for the minimum number of days required before your first expected frost.

**Single-Stemmed Annual Flowers
(one flower per plant, like some sunflowers
and some cockscombs)**

- Note the number of days until your first expected frost.

- Know the number of days required for that specific flower variety to go from seed to bloom.

- To allow for harvest and growth slowdowns, like cool temperatures or fall's short days, add 14 additional days.

- Add the seed-to-bloom days to the additional 14 days for the minimum number of days required before your first expected frost.

I use lightweight row covers to make the winter growing conditions more hospitable, like blocking the cold wind and hiding the plants from hungry creatures.

Cool-Season Hardy Annuals

Cool-season hardy annuals thrive when planted and grown in cool to cold conditions. Because of these awkward planting times, many gardeners skip planting this family, labeling them finicky or thinking they don't grow in their garden's conditions. But the truth is, once we align their cool-season needs with our garden's seasonal growing conditions, this family of plants can become some of the easiest and most abundant flowers in the garden. Cool-season hardy annuals do not have one-size-fits-all planting instructions as warm-season tender annuals do, which are planted once it gets warm and then killed when frost comes. Cool-season annuals have varying planting times, depending on the garden's winter low temperatures. Finding the best planting times for your conditions may take a little time and practice, but it is worth it.

This concept of planting cool-season hardy annuals into cool garden conditions is not new, nor cutting-edge, it is simply a rekindled gardening practice from days gone by. Chances are good that if you had a grandparent or great-grandparent who grew flowers, they knew exactly when and where to plant this family of plants—when air temperatures were cool to cold and into a well-drained garden spot. The story of Steve's grandma planting snap peas around Christmas time on the "high side" of her garden was my first introduction to what cool-season hardy annuals wanted and needed. Grandma knew.

This family of plants will thrive and bloom earlier, with longer stems, and more abundance per plant. You will have plants that are better equipped to face adverse conditions when you align your conditions with their needs.

Cool-Season Notes of Interest

- Poor drainage is a leading cause of plant loss.
- Where summer conditions are cool with low humidity, cool-season plants may bloom throughout summer.
- Plant healthy, vigorous transplants to provide a strong anchor to grow and sit and wait in cool to cold conditions.

Your Cool-Season Planting Windows

Using the dates from page 62–63, fill in this quick reference guide.

Fall planting is 6 to 8 weeks before the first fall expected frost date. My planting window is _____.

Winter planting is anytime during winter when conditions are mild enough that the ground doesn't freeze.

Very early spring planting is 6 to 8 weeks before the last expected spring frost. My planting window is _____.

Planting Time Notes for Cool-Season Hardy Annuals

Fall plant *those flowers that survive your lowest average winter temperatures*. See individual flower pages for winter survival temperatures, starting on page 62–63. The target fall planting time is 6 to 8 weeks before your first expected fall frost date. This 6- to 8-week window before cold winter conditions begin allows transplants to become established or seeds planted in the garden to sprout and grow into a small plant. These young plants will live through winter because their roots have time to grow and become acclimated to their environment during fall's cool but not freezing conditions. When freezing conditions do occur, the plants go dormant, stopping growth to conserve energy and waiting until their preferred conditions return in very early spring. This natural cycle is what leads fall plantings to bloom earlier than very early spring plantings, because the plants are prepared and are ready to restart growing at a moment's notice when weather conditions improve. They already have established roots from fall that can now support their quick growth.

You can fall plant any flower that survives your winter's lowest temperatures to benefit from the resulting strong foundation. Aside from blooming earlier, fall-planted plants also come out of winter well-equipped to offer more abundant blooms with longer stems. They face pests and disease pressures with greater resistance. Fall planting is particularly beneficial for those growing in southern conditions that may experience little to no springlike conditions, going from winter conditions directly into hot and humid summer conditions.

Winter plant *those flowers that survive your lowest winter temperatures*, with conditions mild enough that the ground doesn't freeze. See individual flower pages for winter survival temperatures, starting on page 62–63. Begin planting 6 to 8 weeks before the coolest temperatures of the winter season. Continue throughout winter conditions, with the last planting 6 to 8 weeks before the end of cool conditions. Adjust these timelines, as needed, for your particular winter conditions. Keep

A fall planted cool-season garden that faced several weeks of springlike weather during winter and then it flipped back to cold winter conditions. The garden fared well, but this farmer missed the opportunity to install flower support. It happens.

in mind that planting into the coolest soil and air temperatures is a guiding principle, along with enough cool-season days left for the plants to become established before producing flowers. Mild climates without freezing temperatures have a wide selection of potential flowers to plant, but pinpointing the best planting times may take some trial and error.

Very early spring *is when all cool-season hardy annuals can be planted.* Plant up to 6 to 8 weeks before the last expected spring frost date. This allows the plants to become established in cool to cold conditions before vegetative growth gets started and the growing conditions start to heat up.

   Special note: Planting beds should be prepared in the fall to be completely ready and waiting for that very early spring planting. Often, in late winter and early spring, the soil is too wet, frozen, and even covered in snow to be able to prepare the soil. Cover the prepared area with a silage tarp or other covering that can be pulled back at planting time to reveal the ready-and-waiting bed.

   With the cool-season plants' ability to get the garden started so much earlier, gardeners with short growing seasons or long, frigid winter conditions that prevent fall or winter plantings benefit especially from very early spring plantings. This is also an opportunity for additional plantings of fall-planted flowers to extend the bloom season.

   At this planting time, I find transplanting is best instead of planting seeds in the garden as the cool to cold temperatures significantly delay seeds from sprouting.

Plan Your Garden

Bringing the cutting garden to life with abundant flowering requires keeping a broad view of the process. Don't get lost in the details. Keep repeating these same steps. Keep the plan simple while learning to recognize and manage the garden's lifecycle. Planting more plants of fewer types of flowers makes it easier. A way to add additional diversity to the flower harvest is to grow mixed colors of the flowers planted.

Each of these 16' beds has 5–7 different types of flowers planted in various colors to provide ongoing harvests of diversity.

Planning Your Space for Succession Planting

My first warm-season planting date:

_____

My fall-planted cool-season target date: _____

_____

My very early spring cool-season target date:

_____

Benary's Giant Zinnias are the most commercially grown zinnias by cut-flower growers. Consider more than just the flower when selecting. The plants should have cut-flower qualities like growing tall, long vase life, and prolific production.

Grow Cut Flower Varieties

When I started that first garden in 1998, the only resources available were books and magazine articles about growing cutting gardens. Home computers and the internet were just becoming available, hard to believe, but I think this helped me succeed. I didn't face the endless choices of so many beautiful flowers that we have today, which may or may not be good cut flowers. My limited access kept me focused on those recommended proven cut flowers that ushered me straight into success.

I recommend growing flowers in the cutting garden that are known as good, long-lasting cut flowers. When selecting flower varieties to grow beyond the varieties recommended in this book, look for indications in the plant's description that it is a good cut flower. Websites or catalogs may display the scissors icon indicating it is a cut-flower variety.

Planning Checklist

Mark your dates for:

1 First warm-season planting window:

_____

2 Second warm-season planting window:

_____

3 Fall cool-season planting window:

_____

4 Very early spring cool-season planting window:

_____

5 Count back the number of weeks from the planting dates for seed-starting dates.

_____

6 Count back from the seed-starting date for ordering supplies and seeds.

_____

Go to your garden space:

1 **Measure** the cutting-garden space.

2 **Divide that garden in half** to create two bed spaces for succession plantings.

3 **Measure how many feet** of bed space is in one of those halves.

4 **As a planning guide,** four rows in a 36-inch (90 cm)-wide bed, with plants 6 inches (15 cm) apart in a row.

5 **One foot (30 cm) of bed** will typically support eight plants.

6 **Plan the flowers in each planting** according to the available space.

The Cutting Garden's Lifeline: Harvesting

Harvesting all the flowers that are ready to harvest on a regular basis is the key to plants growing more blooms. Harvesting properly is the one step I see folks skip most often. Developing a harvesting habit will lead to abundance—growing the most flower stems from the garden for the longest period of time.

Why is harvesting so important? Annual plants follow a simple lifecycle. Their purpose in life is to produce a flower that will mature on the plant and go on to grow seeds to scatter in the garden to continue their legacy. When the flower is not harvested, the plant completes this cycle and begins to slow the production of new flowers because its mission in life is accomplished. Interrupting this cycle, by harvesting the flowers, sends the message to the plant to grow more flowers so it can achieve its purpose in life—producing seeds. This simple cycle is the reason annual flower varieties continue to produce flowers as long as the flowers are harvested on a regular basis. It is the simplicity of this lifecycle that makes annual plants the perfect cutting-garden plants.

flower farmer insider tip

CUT FLOWER TRAITS
- Long vase life
- Holds petals
- Tall stems
- Productive
- Strong necks
- Sometimes pollenless

Curveball: Some families of plants may include great cut-flower varieties as well as not-so-good cut-flower varieties. Even though the flowers may look the same, they may have very different individual characteristics. Do the research.

Harvest every flower that is at the harvest stage or beyond. Leave no flowers behind to slow regrowth and clog up your next harvest with old flowers. A cool-season hardy annual spring harvest.

Where to Make the Cut on
Branching Annuals

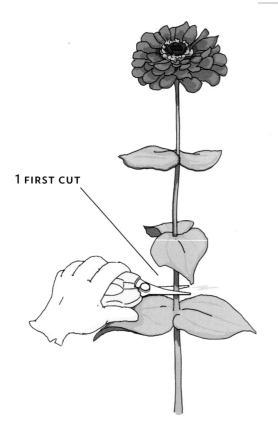

1 FIRST CUT

1 First cut of unpinched branching annual

2 FUTURE CUTS

2 Future cuts at the base of the stem
New stems emerge from where the cut is made.

This illustration shows the proper cutting of a zinnia plant to encourage the most flowers possible. This technique is the same for all branching annuals.

How to Harvest

Go into each harvest knowing you will cut every bloom in this garden at the proper stage to harvest. The only decision is whether the stem is a keeper to go in the harvest bucket or, if blemished, dropped in the pathway. This practice keeps your garden growing and full of only fresh clean blossoms ready and waiting for the next harvest day. For specific harvesting details on individual flowers, see the respective flower profile pages starting on page 66, which also include stages to harvest and any special handling recommendations.

Cut-Flower Stem Care

Once a stem is harvested, the food, water, and hormones that the mother plant provided are no longer available. To help flowers continue to stay healthy in the vase as long as possible and continue opening, I recommended the

Harvesting Tips

- **Harvest twice a week** for the highest production and best quality blooms.

- **Harvest container:** Use a clean, plastic container filled with 2 to 3 inches (5 to 7.5 cm) of water.

- **Use bypass pruning shears** to harvest.

- **Harvest before or after** the heat of the day.

- **During high heat,** the earlier in the day you can harvest the better.

- **Move the harvest container** out of the sun and wind during intense conditions.

- **While harvesting, place flowers** in your hand with the blooms aligned evenly.

- **Cut the stem ends even** once your hand is full.

- **Place the handful in the bucket** with stems standing upright.

- **Group the same flower types together** in the container to prevent crushing.

- **Move the harvest container indoors** to a cool spot.

- **Allow the flowers to recover** after harvest for at least 4 hours, overnight preferred, before working with them.

ABOVE, FROM LEFT *As I harvest, I strip the foliage from the stem, and lay the stem in my hand keeping the blooms fairly even until my hand is full, and then cut the stems even as I make my way to the harvest bucket. This helps to prevent crushing blooms in the bucket.*

Place each handful in the bucket upright and as straight as possible. As you add more stems, the easier they stand up. Using the appropriately sized harvest container for the volume of stems makes this easy.

Ethylene Gas Damage

Cut flowers exposed to ethylene gas can suffer premature dropped leaves, buds, and flowers, among other symptoms. Flowers sensitive to ethylene gas are noted on the Flower Feature pages. Avoid common sources of ethylene gas in a home, like vegetables, fruit, and cigarette smoke. Flower farmers should store only flowers in coolers and keep the cooler floors clear of plant debris that can give off ethylene gas as it ages.

following flower conditioning products and steps. These steps will increase the flowers' vase life by controlling bacteria growth, providing nutrition, promoting water absorption, and regulating water pH. I follow product package directions.

CONDITIONING PRODUCTS (Resources on page 230)

- **Chlorine tablets** in harvest container to kill bacteria

- **Holding solution** in the container when holding flowers more than 48 hours before use; this slows development yet provides necessary nutrition and sanitation

- **Fresh-cut flower food** in vases to control bacteria, provide nutrition, promote water absorption, and regulate water pH

- **Hydrating solution** to prevent or correct drooping by boosting water uptake

CONDITIONING STEPS

All harvest containers get a chlorine tablet, and cut flowers are allowed to rest in it for at least 4 hours following harvest. The next steps:

- **Home garden:** Use fresh-cut flower food in the vase.

- **Flower farmer:** If holding flowers for more than 48 hours or delivering to a commercial customer, transfer the flowers into holding solution.

Troubleshooting

- **Drooping blooms:** Recut stems 2 inches (5 cm) and use **hydrating solution**.

- **Wilted foliage:** Strip foliage as recommended to prevent wilting and, if needed, use **hydrating solution** to correct.

- **Bent flowers:** Use a taller, narrower container to keep tall stems straight; use the appropriate-size container for the volume and stem length during harvest and holding.

flower farmer insider tip

Meet the Dirty Dozen Flowers. The "Dirty Dozen Flowers" earned their name by polluting vase water faster than other flowers, plus they are more sensitive to pollution in general. Their stems dump organic matter, enzymes, and carbs into the water as they heal the harvest cut. This debris triggers a bacterial explosion that begins when the stem hits the surface of the water. Bacteria lead to a shorter vase life and cloudy water. Chlorine tablets prevent and delay bacterial growth.

1 Amaranth
2 Bachelor button
3 Calendula
4 Celosia
5 Feverfew
6 Marigold
7 Ornamental kale
8 Snapdragon
9 Stock
10 Sunflower
11 Yarrow
12 Zinnia

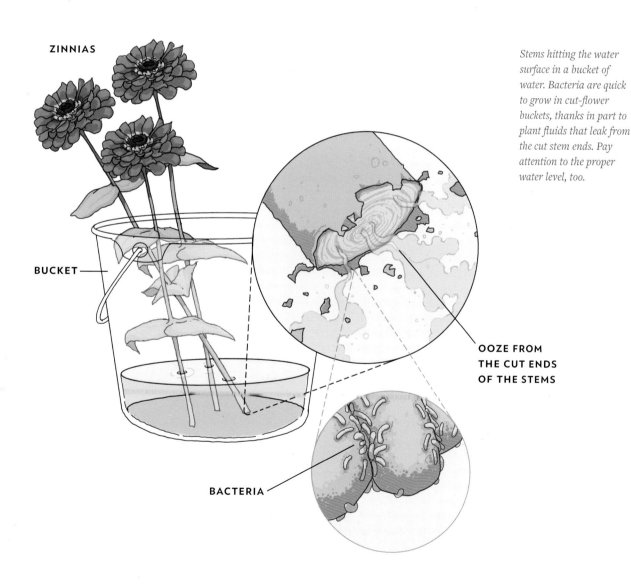

ZINNIAS

BUCKET

Stems hitting the water surface in a bucket of water. Bacteria are quick to grow in cut-flower buckets, thanks in part to plant fluids that leak from the cut stem ends. Pay attention to the proper water level, too.

OOZE FROM THE CUT ENDS OF THE STEMS

BACTERIA

two

The Basics of Growing Cut Flowers

DURING THE TIME I TRANSITIONED from a home gardener to a flower farmer, I learned about gardening methods and supplies I had never seen before, and my eyes were opened to more efficient and cost-effective ways to care for my cutting gardens.

Although you may not want to grow cut flowers to sell, following the steps that flower farmers take will help you grow a garden you can spend more time enjoying than doing chores in. These methods are easily applied to any size garden and make gardening as simple and easy as possible while growing an abundance of beautiful cut flowers.

Best Bed Location and Preparation

The day-to-day care, health of the plants, and the flowers produced are impacted by the physical location of the cutting garden. Consider these tips before selecting a spot.

Full sun: 8 to 10 hours of sunlight daily is required for a cutting garden to remain in top-producing condition. The plants in this highly productive garden will regrow new shoots and remain healthy with the maximum amount of sunlight available. Placing this garden in a low-light spot will slow regrowth and can encourage disease and pests.

Freestanding: A freestanding, dedicated bed accessible from all sides is recommended. Scattering cut-flower plantings among landscape beds makes it challenging to provide flower support and to stay on top of chores. Beds located against structures may block sunlight, can be difficult to install flower support in, and impair harvesting with a potential longer reach into the bed.

A small space, when treated as a cutting garden, produces a lot of beautiful cut flowers.

Recommended Bed Sizes

The recommended bed sizes for a three-season cutting garden are:

Home garden: 2 beds, each 3 × 10 feet (0.9 × 3 m)

Flower enthusiast: 2 beds, each 3 × 16 feet (0.9 × 5 m)

Budding flower farmer: 8 beds, each 3 × 50 feet (0.9 × 15 m)

Out of sight: Placing this garden out of sight solves a common challenge new cut-flower gardeners face—they can't bring themselves to cut the flowers! The two most common reasons that hold them back are that they enjoy looking at the garden from a relaxing spot, or they fear that the flowers will not regrow. Locating this garden behind a garage or in an underused side yard will help overcome the gazing-at-the-garden problem. For those who fear that the flowers will not regrow, follow the instructions in this book and they will grow, I promise.

Water source: Consider the location of your water source. Although the recommended plants are drought tolerant once established, they will need supplemental watering throughout the seasons and especially immediately after planting. Dragging a heavy hose a long distance in the heat of summer, when water may be most needed, discourages routine watering (see irrigation recommendations, page 40).

Bed Size

How big? Even after two and half decades of being a commercial cut-flower grower, I am still floored by the volume of flowers my little flower farm produces each week. Harvesting the garden at least once a week, with twice a week being optimal, keeps this garden producing. When a cutting garden is larger and produces more abundance than the need, it leads us to slow harvesting; the plants, in turn, slow regrowing. Looking back, my most productive years per square foot were when I grew a smaller garden than I thought I needed. Why grow in four beds when two beds, tended as cutting gardens, can produce as much, if not more?

Width and length: The length of the beds depends some on the need, but the width plays a role in helping or hindering harvesting and chores. Narrower beds are easier to reach into the center of and low where the harvest cut is made helps prevent us from stepping on the bed during harvesting. A 36-inch (90 cm)-wide bed works well, with my beds getting narrower as I age to reduce the reaching and bending distance. My beds now are 30 inches (75 cm) wide, and I plant the same recommended number of rows in each bed and use same row spacing as 36-inch (90 cm)-wide beds throughout this book.

Preparing the Beds

I grow in raised beds because it is easier to improve drainage and soil quality. Beds can have either framed sides made with lumber or just mounded soil with no framed sides. Some advantages of planting in a raised bed include the soil warming faster, less soil compaction in the bed, and better drainage. If you face poor soil conditions, like heavy clay, raised beds are a great way to overcome the problem. During cool to cold conditions, garden beds may stay wet longer, which can lead to rot and disease. Raised beds dry out more quickly naturally.

I grow in both framed and mounded raised beds. My commercial beds are mounded, and I have two 16-foot (5 m) beds that have frames made from three high cedar 6 × 6-inch (15 × 15 cm) lumber. The framed beds are easy

My commercial mounded-type raised beds made with my tractor and a bedmaker implement using biodegradable mulch film. I built film-covered beds with a walk-behind tiller and a shovel for my first decade of farming.

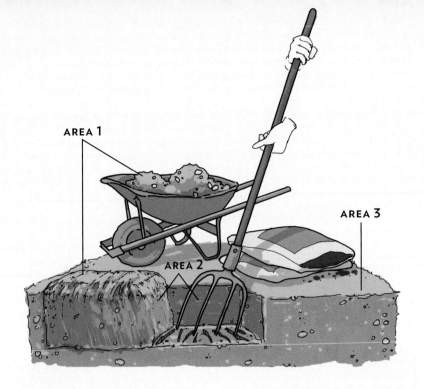

AREA 1

AREA 2

AREA 3

An easy way to dig a new mounded bed. Area #1 has been lifted into the wheelbarrow and cracks made in the bottom. Area #2 has been lifted onto area #1 and the bottom of #2 is ready to have cracks made. Area #3 is untouched and will be lifted next.

Making a Mounded Raised Bed from Scratch

1   Remove any vegetation growing in the area.

2   You'll need a garden fork, garden spade or shovel, wheelbarrow, compost to cover the entire bed with 6 to 8 inches (15 to 20 cm), and general-purpose dry organic fertilizer.

3   Standing at the end of the bed on a long side, use the garden spade to lift out the width of the spade, going no more than 6 inches (15 cm) deep, working across the 36-inch (90 cm)-wide bed. Place the strip of soil in the wheelbarrow. Set the wheelbarrow aside.

4   Place the garden fork into the bed where the strip was just removed and step on the fork, pushing it as deep as possible. Rock the fork back and forth cracking open the soil, but not removing the soil. Pull the fork out, move a few inches, and repeat. Do this throughout the area where the strip was removed.

5   Put 2 to 4 inches (5 to 10 cm) of compost on top of the cracks you just created in the soil.

6   Step to the right and lift out the next strip of soil; place this soil to your left on top of the compost just added.

7   Repeat steps 4 and 5 and continue this process to the end of the bed.

8   In the last open strip, and after adding the compost, dump in the soil from the wheelbarrow.

9   According to the package directions, sprinkle the dry organic fertilizer over the bed's surface.

10   Top the entire bed with 2 to 4 inches (5 to 10 cm) of compost, incorporating it all, and breaking up any dirt clogs to create the planting surface.

11   Shape the bed top with a slight depression in the center to prevent quick water runoff.

12   The result is raised bed with improved drainage. If you prevent bed soil compaction by not stepping on the bed, this process does not need to be repeated (see replanting notes, page 55).

to maintain and tidy in appearance, and their height makes chores easy. The mounded beds require more tending but are my preferred method in a high-production farming garden.

Don't let poor soil conditions keep you from getting started. Following the bed building recommendations and the replanting steps will work toward improving soil conditions at each planting (see page 55). Using natural amendments such as compost along with organic fertilizers will improve the soil with each passing season. Organic matter holds water like a sponge yet improves drainage so excess water drains away. Improving soil conditions is an ongoing part of the life of your garden.

Make a Framed Quick-and-Easy Bed from Scratch

My cedar raised beds are 18-inches tall and the 6-inch-wide frame makes for a convenient spot to sit and work.

1 Cut the vegetation in the bed area as low as possible or remove it.

2 Have on hand the bed frame of choice, cardboard to cover the ground inside the frame, potting soil and compost to make a 50/50 mix and to fill the frame, and dry organic fertilizer. Large bales of potting soil may be available from your local nursery or farm supply store.

3 Place the bed frame on the area and level it.

4 Using a garden fork, work through the bed area: Step on the fork, drive it in as deep as possible, and rock the tool to create cracks and openings in the soil to improve drainage.

5 Place a layer of overlapping cardboard in the bed to cover the entire area to smoother vegetation.

6 Fill the frame with the potting soil and compost, mixing it 50/50 as you add it.

7 According to the package directions, apply and incorporate the dry organic fertilizer throughout the bed.

8 Shape the bed top with a slight depression in the center to prevent quick water runoff and keep the soil level 2 inches (5 cm) below the frame.

The head of a bed with T-tape irrigation installed. I often lay woven landscape cloth across the head of a garden to create a vegetation free area for the irrigation header. We use a string trimmer to maintain the edge of the fabric.

Garden Bed Irrigation

Garden irrigation saves water, and money, and grows healthier plants. It delivers the water at ground level where it is needed on the roots and prevents water loss from evaporation. Low-pressure irrigation systems like driplines and T-tape are long lasting, easy to install, and use little water. Frequency of watering is determined by monitoring the soil and weather conditions.

To learn what type of irrigation fits your garden, soil conditions, layout, and water source, I recommend exploring the irrigation sources in the Resources section (page 230). They offer tutorial videos and customer support, along with supplies and irrigation kits for backyard gardens to farm-size fields.

Weed Prevention

Learning that weed prevention should be addressed long before weeds are even seen saved my flower-farming life. Little did I know I was helping weed seeds sprout and grow by the way I was prepping and planting my beds, and no matter how hard I worked, I couldn't outpace the vigorously growing weeds. But, then I learned the missing piece that changed it all: Preventing weed seeds from sprouting would prevent the whole process and problem.

Where do all the weed seeds come from? Weed seeds survive a long time, sometimes decades, waiting for the opportunity to sprout. Add this to the fact that some weed plants can produce a million seeds per plant and it is easy to see why there are so many weeds. My best weed prevention steps are to keep weed seeds from sprouting, and prevent those that do get away from me and sprout from growing to produce more seeds to fuel future weed pressure.

Each time the soil is disturbed, like when preparing beds, fresh weed seeds are brought to the soil's surface. Once on or nearer the surface, they get what they need to sprout: sunlight and favorable soil temperatures. Interrupting this process by either mulching or cultivating can prevent them from sprouting. Planting in permanent beds with minimal soil disturbance will limit the number of weed seeds brought to the surface and, ultimately, reduces the weed seed population over time.

Weeds that spread by runners, on the other hand, grow from underground roots. Pulling the top vegetation and the roots near the surface in an effort to remove the plant as we would a weed plant that grew from a seed, tends to encourage additional growth from the roots. Removing all the roots or treating the plants with organic or nonorganic herbicide according to the package directions to kill the roots/runners coupled with follow-up weed preventative care will help prevent the weed plant from creeping back into the garden.

The problem with allowing any weed plants to grow in your beds is that they compete with the favored plants for water, nutrition, and the space needed to grow. Another significant problem with weeds growing in the bed is they can quickly mature to scatter seeds in the garden to perpetuate their lifecycle.

I follow different methods of weed prevention for transplant and seed plantings in the garden. The steps and timing for both are essential to preventing as many weeds as possible.

flower farmer insider tip

WEED TRUTHS
- Prevention is key.
- Weeds do grow in cool to cold conditions.
- There is NO permanent weed solution.
- Out-of-control weeds this year plant the seeds for next season.

WEED PREVENTION IN THE GARDEN WHEN PLANTING SEEDS

Planting seeds outdoors in the garden is called *direct sowing*. I direct sow into garden beds with no mulch to allow for easy cultivation with a garden hoe. Seeds are planted just after preparing the soil or disturbing the soil surface to interrupt any developing weed seeds. This disruption gives the weed seeds and the flower seeds an equal start on sprouting.

For the quickest cultivation, I plant three rows of seeds per bed instead of four when planting transplants. Begin hoeing 14 days from the seed-sowing date and continue biweekly. I use my garden hoe throughout the surface, *between the rows of seeds sown*. The easiest elimination happens when weed seedlings are microscopic—hoe even if you don't see them yet. Using a true garden hoe with the blade attached to the handle at the proper angle makes this job comfortable and fast (see Resources, page 230).

Stop hoeing chores once the plant canopy begins to shade the bed's surface or below-freezing conditions start. Mulching the area between rows is optional once the seedlings have reached 5 inches (13 cm) or more in height.

PLANTING TRANSPLANTS IN THE GARDEN ALLOWS MULCHING

Years of mulching with leaves, shredded bark, compost, and straw have suppressed billions of weed seeds and contributed to building my soil. I use a mix of mulching methods, selecting the method that is practical at a particular planting time. Using so many different types of mulch has given me a long-term glimpse of how mulching contributes to and protects the soil as well as of its other benefits. Mulching changed the way I planned my garden, the steps I followed, and the timing of those steps.

What is mulch? Mulch is a protective covering placed on the soil's surface. It can be organic plant material like bark, pine straw, and leaves, or it can be a man-made product, like plastic, weed barrier fabric, or biodegradable film. Each type of mulch covers the soil to block light to suppress weed seeds from sprouting, and each has its pros and cons. I base my choice on what is available at the time of planting, the cost, and how it affects the health of my garden.

Applying mulch immediately after disturbing the soil is highly effective to block light from the soil's surface to prevents weed seeds from sprouting.

FROM FAR LEFT *Before planting seeds directly in the garden, use a garden rake to disturb the top 1 to 2 inches (2.5 to 5 cm) of previously prepared soil to interrupt any developing weed seedlings, even if they're not visible yet. This gives your flower seeds and the weed seeds an even starting time.*

This style of garden hoe works pain-free and efficiently, allowing you to stand up straight with the blade flat on the ground in the working position. Using a continuous pulling motion and keeping the blade flat, pull the blade through the top 1 to 2 inches (2.5 to 5 cm) of soil to extinguish developing weed seeds. This only disturbs the top few inches of soil and prevents bringing up additional weed seeds lurking deeper in the soil. After several hoeings, the weed seed population on the surface is depleted.

A very early spring planting of cool-season hardy annuals already in with additional empty beds ready, warming, and waiting for the first spring planted warm-season tender annuals.

Delaying mulching by even a few days after soil disturbance has a different result: Weed seeds get enough of a head start, even though not visible yet, and are strong enough to push through mulch once applied. By mulching immediately following the soil's disturbance, the seeds continue to lay dormant, and most weeds are prevented.

My go-to method is to plant transplants into mulched beds. This allows mulch to be applied immediately following the bed preparation regardless of whether the transplants are ready to be planted. Beds can be made and mulched to sit and wait for the planting without weed seeds sprouting.

Why I Mulch

- Suppresses weed growth
- Regulates soil temperature
- Prevents erosion
- Retains moisture
- Encourages beneficial creatures working the soil
- Organic mulches provide nutrients as they breakdown

A fall planted transplanted bed that is covered with biodegradable film with pathways 8 to 12 inches (20 to 30 cm) deep of leaf mulch. No soil is exposed to allow weed seeds to get the light they need to sprout.

WHICH MULCH?

There is no one-size-fits-all conditions for mulch. The type of mulch I use is based on whether it is the cool season or the warm season and what type of mulch is available. For instance, I find biodegradable mulch film works best for cool-season hardy annual transplant beds. It has the strongest weed suppression during the time that these transplants grow slowly, but cool-season weeds seem to grow quickly. The film blocks sunlight from the entire bed surface except the small hole made for the transplant, minimizing the area weed seeds can sprout. To get this type of weed suppression with an organic mulch in a cool-season bed, the mulch would have to be deep and dense and could easily suffocate young transplants. My preferred mulching practices are:

COOL SEASON

- **Transplanted beds** are covered with biodegradable mulch film, black-side up to help warm the soil, with pathways mulched with leaves.

- **Seeds planted on bed tops** left bare, with pathways mulched with leaves.

WARM SEASON

- **Transplanted beds** are covered with organic mulch or with biodegradable mulch film, gray- or white-side up to cool the bed surface in hot conditions. Pathways grow native vegetation and are mowed weekly.

- **Seeds planted on bed tops** left bare, with pathways allowed to grow vegetation to mow weekly. I do not plant warm-season seeds directly into the garden because of my strong weed pressure. Planting transplants is less work with better results.

TYPES OF MULCH I USE
Organic

- **Tree leaves:** Excellent pathway covering, free, available in fall and winter, shredding not required for pathway use; 10 to 12 inches (25 to 30 cm) deep, habitat for beneficial creatures, good moisture retention, and feeds the soil as they break down. Shredded leaves and leaf mold are good to use on bed tops.

- **Wood bark:** Prefer shredded; good to use on permanent beds and pathways; more labor to spread, 2 to 4 inches (5 to 10 cm) deep.

- **Compost:** Excellent to use on bed tops, 2 to 4 inches (5 to 10 cm) deep.

Inorganic

- **Biodegradable mulch film:** Looks like plastic but is biodegradable, made from a plant-based bioplastic that breaks down in 4 to 6 months; can be incorporated into the soil after use or left on the surface to break down; easy to plant through; can be used alone or under organic mulch to block light; available with a black side and gray or white side for surface temperature control.

Direct-sown bells of Ireland bed with leaved pathways. I like to wait until seeds have sprouted and reached 3 to 5 inches (7.5 to 13 cm) before mulching the pathways because the leaves work their way onto the bed tops from the wind.

Starting from Seed Indoors and in the Garden

The best reason to start your flowers from seed is to have access to healthy cut-flower variety transplants at their proper planting time. There are two basic ways to start seeds: Plant seeds outdoors in the garden where they will grow to maturity, or start the seeds indoors to grow into a transplant that is then planted outdoors in the garden when it is 3 to 5 inches (7.5 to 13 cm) tall. There are pros and cons for each and several methods for each.

Which way to start a seed should begin with the way the seed prefers: indoors or outdoors? The suggested method on seed packets is based on which way provides the conditions that make sprouting successful. If this information is not on the seed packet, enter into a search engine, "How to start [flower name] seeds?"

When the directions suggest that a seed can be started indoors or outdoors, I always chose indoors. Here is why: After starting millions of seeds on my farm, I have been more successful starting seeds indoors instead of planting seeds directly into the garden. Planting seeds outdoors in the elements requires intense care and often on the ground doing tasks like thinning, watering, and weed control. Compare that process to starting indoors, which requires daily watering in a comfortable environment with no thinning or weeding chores required. Starting indoors has been less work.

My seed-starting setup and garden conditions have led me to start all warm-season tender annual seeds indoors and to plant seeds in the garden of only a few cool-season hardy annuals that perform best that way. How I start each can be found on the Flower Feature pages starting on page 66. For those flowers that can be started either way, I list my preferred way first.

RIGHT *Seed come in many ways: raw or coated with a yellow clay material for easier planting, and even treated. 1. Zinnias raw and coated 2. Sunflowers raw and treated 3. Scabiosa raw and still in chaff 4. Marigolds raw and coated 5. Celosia raw and coated.*

FAR RIGHT *One of my grow room racks setups with grow lights. Each shelf can support 750 ¾" size soil block seedlings, each 48" long x 18" wide stand holds 4,500 transplants.*

Sowing bachelor button seeds into the trough, placing a seed every 1 inch or so. Planting in troughs helps to direct water only to the flower seeds and gives a visual cue of where the seeds were planted.

Planting Seeds in the Garden

1 Plant seeds into bare soil.

2 Sow in straight rows for easy cultivation and identification.

3 Using your hand, draw a straight line on the soil surface making a "V" trough, 1 to 2 inches (2.5 to 5 cm) deep to plant the seeds.

4 Plant the seeds by sprinkling a seed on the bottom of the trough every 1 inch (2.5 cm).

5 Cover the seed with soil, or not, according to the package instructions.

6 Water and keep moist until sprouting.

7   Watering only in the troughs helps prevent weed seeds from sprouting throughout the bed.

8   Once seedlings reach 3 to 5 inches (7.5 to 13 cm) tall, thin to the recommended spacing.

9   For preventing weeds, see page 40.

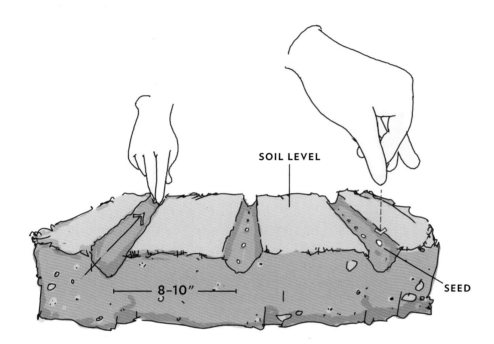

SOIL LEVEL

8–10"

SEED

Create troughs with your hands, then plant the seeds.

Sowing Cool-Season Hardy Annual Seeds in the Garden

For flowers that prefer to have their seeds sown in the garden and survive your winter's lowest temperature, fall sowing is the best choice. However, if that flower would not survive your winter's lowest temperature, the window to plant is very early spring, which is 6 to 8 weeks before the last spring frost. The challenge with sowing seeds outdoors in the garden at this time is that it is usually too cold to encourage seeds to sprout. To overcome this, either push the outdoor sowing date closer to the last expected frost or sprout the seeds indoors in a cool location in soil blocks and plant outdoors immediately following sprouting.

Starting Seeds Indoors with Soil Blocking

My go-to soil blocking tools:

1. Swift Blocker Mini 27

2. Swift Blocker Mini 75

3. Swift Scraper/Seeder

4. Ladbrooke ¾" Blocker

5. Ladbrooke 2" Blocker

6. Ladbrooke inserts for the 2" blocker.

1 Fill the soil blocker chambers with wet blocking mix.

2 Scrape excess mix off the bottom.

3 Squeeze the plunger to make the blocks.

4 Sow one seed per block with a moistened toothpick.

5 Place blocks on a seedling heat mat and keep blocks evenly moist.

6 Lay wide-weave burlap on blocks during sprouting to retain moisture and allow air circulation. Remove when sprouting begins.

7 To water, pour a gentle stream into the tray daily. Wait a few moments and pour off any standing water. Once a week, add liquid organic fertilizer to the water according to the package directions.

8 Move the tray from the seedling heat mat to a grow light once 50 percent of the seeds start sprouting.

9 Move outdoors to get acclimated to conditions for a few days before planting. Protect blocks from direct rain.

10 Plant in the garden once 3 to 5 inches (7.5 to 13 cm) tall.

NOTES:

- Soil blocker size recommendation on Flower Feature pages starting on page 66.
- See Resources (page 230) for seed-starting supplies and resources.

Planting sunflower seeds in a 128-cell plug tray. Sunflower seeds prefer to be covered with soil for the best germination. During watering, the soil on the walls of the cells will wash down to complete the cover the seeds with soil.

Starting Seeds Indoors in Cell Trays (for Large Seeds, Like Sunflowers)

1 Fill the tray with a 50/50 mix of potting soil and compost.

2 Drop one seed per cell on the surface.

3 Using your finger, push the seed down into the cell about 1 inch (2.5 cm).

4 Water well and allow the tray to drain.

5 Place the tray on a seedling heat mat and keep evenly moist.

6 Move the tray from the mat to a grow light once 50 percent of the seeds have sprouted, or outdoors if conditions are favorable.

7 Plant in the garden once 3 to 5 inches (7.5 to 13 cm) tall, which normally takes 2–3 weeks.

8 See Resources (page 230) for seed-starting supplies and resources.

Pinching Plants

"Pinching" is the term used to describe removing part of a plant right above a set of leaves to induce early branching. Only those plant varieties that have a branching habit are candidates for pinching. Keeping in mind that some flower families have both branching and nonbranching varieties, like sunflowers and cockscomb, verify what you are growing before you pinch.

Pinching plants early in their lifecycle results in a plant producing three or four good, usable stems as the first flush as well as continuing to produce additional stems. Plants not pinched will bloom earlier because that central stem was not removed and, in fact, its first harvest cut acts as the pinch that also induces branching (as shown in the harvest illustration, page 30).

My preference is to follow a 50/50 pinching practice to get the best of both worlds. I pinch half of the plants in each variety, so I get the earliest blooms possible from the unpinched plants, followed by the pinched plants' abundant flush of blooms.

The two rows of marigolds on the right were pinched 10 days after planting to encourage earlier branching while the two rows on the left were not pinched and will bloom earlier.

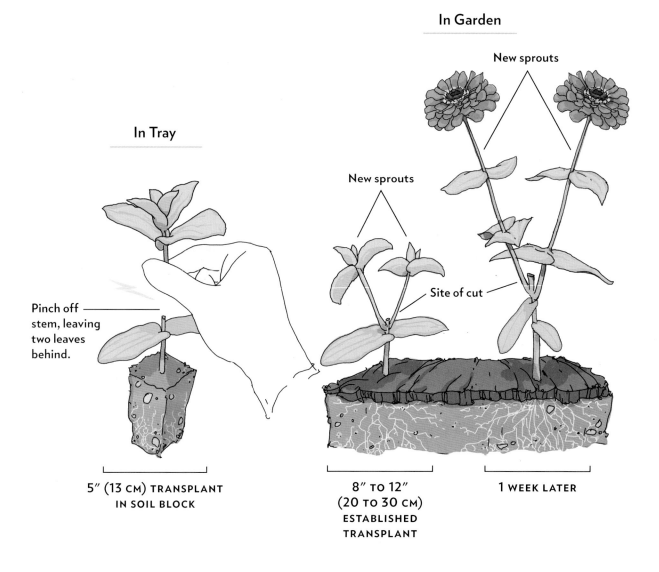

In Garden

New sprouts

In Tray

New sprouts

Pinch off stem, leaving two leaves behind.

Site of cut

5" (13 CM) TRANSPLANT IN SOIL BLOCK

8" TO 12" (20 TO 30 CM) ESTABLISHED TRANSPLANT

1 WEEK LATER

PINCHING

- Pinch plants while still in the tray 7 to 10 days *before* **planting them** into the garden. Watch for tiny sprouts at the pinch site as a sign they have recovered and are ready for transplanting into the garden. Pinching in the tray can save the day when a tray can't be planted on time and is outgrowing its space.

- **Pinch plants 7 to 10 days** *after* **planting in the garden,** which allows plants to recover before pinching.

- **Transplants 5 inches (13 cm) or taller can be pinched.**

Planting and Caring
for the Cutting Garden

Tight spacing reflects that cutting-garden plants are harvested throughout the season, which is similar to hard pruning each week. Other benefits of close spacing are that it encourages stems to grow taller and straighter, produces more stems from a given space, and the dense canopy of foliage helps outcompete weed pressure.

Continue building the soil by adding 2 to 3 inches (5 to 7.5 cm) of compost and dry organic general-purpose fertilizer according to the package directions each time you replant. I follow two methods after removing the previous planting: I incorporate the fertilizer in the top few inches of soil and lay compost on the surface to use as mulch, and I plant transplants through it, or if soil conditions need improving more quickly, I incorporate the compost along with the fertilizer into the top few inches, mulch, and plant the transplants.

For precise plant spacing, use plastic mesh flower support netting that has 6-inch (15 cm) openings as a planting guide. Roll out the netting onto the bed, pull it out flat, secure it with weights, and plant according to recommendations. The netting is removed immediately when the planting is completed (see Resources, page 230, for netting).

Support the Flowers

Heavy canopies of blooms and buds benefit from flower support to stay upright during rain and wind. A cutting garden laying down broken and dirty after a rainstorm is heartbreaking and, most often, preventable.

Flower support is most effective when installed at the halfway point of the plant's mature height, a 48-inch (120 cm)-tall mature plant's support should be at 24 inches (60 cm). Install the support while the planting is still shorter than the recommended height of its support. This allows stems to grow through the support naturally and the netting almost disappears visually.

Start by installing the netting at one end of the bed and pulling the netting taut from side to side. Go to the other end of the bed and pull the netting taut from the bed both end to end and side to side. Next, install all the stakes along one side of the bed, considering where the opposite stake will fall on the bed and making sure it will be taut and that the stake will be in the bed, not the pathway. Install the stakes on the other side of the bed, pulling the netting taut from side to side.

I use one layer of plastic flower support netting because it provides effective support, is quick and easy to install, and is reusable. Install it using sturdy wooden or metal garden stakes. It is held in place by being pulled taut. The key to removal and reuse is removing it while the bed

BELOW, FROM LEFT
Netting height is at half point of the plant's mature height, 48" tall plants have netting at 24" and so on. Plants quickly grow up through the netting to make it almost invisible.

I prefer netting to be the same width or a little narrower than the bed and for the staking to be in the bed, not in the pathway.

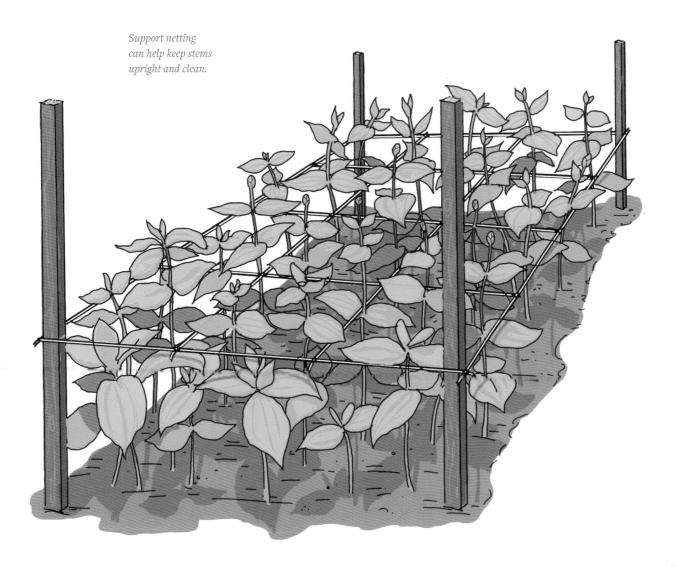

has little vegetative growth above the netting (due to heavy harvesting or deadheading) and before weed pressure begins to develop in the absence of a dense flower canopy. Support recommendations are found on individual Flower Feature pages starting on page 66; netting sources can be found in the Resources section (page 230).

Fertilization

As part of my bed preparation steps, I add general-purpose dry organic fertilizer according to the package directions at each planting. Beyond this and soil amendments like compost, I don't add nutrients without a soil test indicating it is needed. Growing crops like cut flowers can deplete soil nutrients, which can lead to overall poor performance in the garden. Annual soil tests in late summer are optimal to monitor soil conditions and correct deficiencies.

Support netting can help keep stems upright and clean.

Individual flower recommendations beyond the standard bed preparation applications can be found on the Flower Feature pages starting on page 66. For those flowers that benefit from additional applications, I use organic liquid fertilizer applied according to the package directions and run it through the drip irrigation, spray it on the foliage as a foliar feeding, or pour it onto the soil as a soil drench.

Pest and Disease Controls

The best pest and disease control is prevention through healthy growing conditions, avoiding flowers that attract pests and diseases in your growing conditions, and always keeping an eye out for potential problems. However, positive identification is crucial before any steps are taken. Early intervention and proper ID give the best options, like giving Mother Nature a helping hand to resolve a problem rather than ignoring the damage, allowing it to get worse, then panicking and resorting to potentially harmful treatments. I use books, internet searches, and my state's university-based agricultural center for diagnosing and identifying problems. My garden has grown without pesticides and other treatments, including organic products, for over a decade (find recommended books in the Resources section, page 230).

Row Cover

Row cover is a fabric made for outdoor use that helps protect plantings from weather conditions, insects, and varmints, but allows air, water, and light to pass through. I use the lightest weight, which is 0.55 ounce (16 g) per square yard and allows 85 percent light transmission, providing 4°F (about 2°C) of temperature protection to enhance my garden's growing conditions. It can be used in cold and warm conditions and, if additional frost protection is needed, you can use a double layer. Remove covers when snow or frozen precipitation is expected and vent for use in warm weather to prevent overheating (see Resources, page 230).

I use low tunnels with lightweight fabric covers to shelter plantings I want to protect for more than a couple weeks. Hooping the bed with wire supports, a lightweight cover, and securing the cover, creates a cozy growing environment for plants. The covers are used to enhance growing conditions, like concentrating sunshine and blocking wind, but the planting does not depend on the cover for survival; it merely improves the quality of their conditions.

I use lightweight row cover two ways: short term without hoops for newly sown seeds I want to protect from birds and for extended uses like overwintering I use with hoops. Hold covers down with sandbag-type weights with fifteen pounds of soil, sand, or gravel to secure the covers without damage. Place two to three weights at each end of bed and one every 10 feet along the side of the bed or at the foot of each hoop placed every 10 feet.

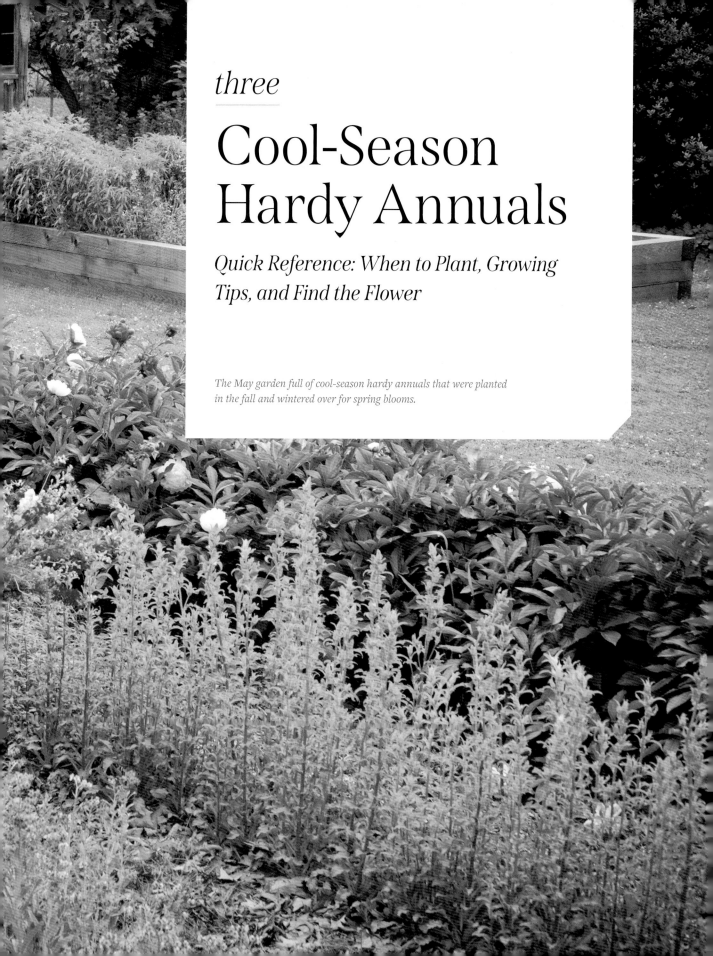

three

Cool-Season Hardy Annuals

Quick Reference: When to Plant, Growing Tips, and Find the Flower

The May garden full of cool-season hardy annuals that were planted in the fall and wintered over for spring blooms.

My Cool-Season Planting Guide

Use this information to plan seed-starting and -planting dates.

My winter lowest temperature:

_____

My first expected fall frost date:

_____

My last expected spring frost date:

_____

PLANT COOL-SEASON HARDY ANNUALS in the garden during the cool to cold conditions of fall and/or very early spring.

Determining when to plant a specific cool-season plant is based on your area's lowest winter temperature and the cold tolerance of the specific plant. For example, if a plant survives your area's lowest winter temperatures, it can be fall planted to winter over. If it does not survive your area's lowest winter temperatures, then plant it in very early spring. Fall plantings can be repeated in very early spring to extend the harvest. For more, see "Planting Warm and Cool Annuals" (page 15).

The fall planting window is 6 to 8 weeks before your historical first expected fall frost. The very early spring planting is 6 to 8 weeks before your historical last expected spring frost.

Find the Flower

PAGE NUMBER	COMMON NAME	BOTANICAL NAME	WINTER LOW TEMPERATURE SURVIVAL
122	Baby's breath	*Gypsophila elegans*	10°F (-12°C)
92	Bachelor button	*Centaurea cyanus*	0°F (-18°C)
134	Bells of Ireland	*Moluccella laevis*	10°F (-12°C)
104	Billy balls	*Craspedia globosa*	10°F (-12°C)
151	Black-eyed Susan	*Rudbeckia hirta, Rudbeckia triloba*	-20°F (-29°C)
83	Bupleurum	*Bupleurum rotundifolium*	-10°F (-23°C)
89	Canterbury bells	*Campanula medium*	-10°F (-23°C)
110	Carnation	*Dianthus caryophyllus*	-10°F (-23°C)
107	Chinese forget-me-not	*Cynoglossum amabile*	0°F (-18°C)
69	Corn cockle	*Agrostemma githago*	10°F (-12°C)
168	Dill	*Anethum graveolens*	10°F (-12°C)
168	False Queen Anne's lace	*Ammi majus, Ammi visnaga*	10°F (-12°C)

PAGE NUMBER	COMMON NAME	BOTANICAL NAME	WINTER LOW TEMPERATURE SURVIVAL
162	Feverfew	*Tanacetum parthenium*	-10°F (-23°C)
114	Foxglove	*Digitalis purpurea*	-10°F (-23°C)
98	Godetia	*Clarkia amoena, Clarkia unguiculata*	20°F (-7°C)
95	Honeywort	*Cerinthe major*	10°F (-12°C)
137	Hybrid bee balm	*Monarda hybrida*	10°F (-12°C)
101	Larkspur	*Consolida ajacis*	0°F (-18°C)
117	Lisianthus	*Eustoma grandiflorum*	0°F (-18°C)
140	Love-in-a-mist	*Nigella damascena*	0°F (-18°C)
80	Ornamental Cabbage	*Brassica oleracea*	10°F (-12°C)
159	Pincushion flower	*Scabiosa atropurpurea*	10°F (-12°C)
146	Poppy	*Papaver nudicaule, Papaver somniferum*	0°F (-18°C)
86	Pot marigold	*Calendula officinalis*	10°F (-12°C)
168	Queen Anne's lace	*Daucus carota*	10°F (-12°C)
75	Snapdragon	*Antirrhinum majus*	0°F (-18°C)
156	Soapwort	*Saponaria vaccaria hispanica*	10°F (-12°C)
159	Starflower	*Scabiosa stellata*	10°F (-12°C)
128	Statice	*Limonium sinuatum*	20°F (-7°C)
131	Stock	*Matthiola incana*	20°F (-7°C)
171	Strawflower	*Xerochrysum bracteatum*	10°F (-12°C)
125	Sweet pea	*Lathyrus odoratus*	10°F (-12°C)
110	Sweet William	*Dianthus barbatus*	-10°F (-23°C)
165	Throatwort	*Trachelium caeruleum*	20°F (-7°C)
143	White lace flower	*Orlaya grandiflora*	-5°F (-20.5°C)
72	Winged everlasting	*Ammobium alatum*	20°F (-7°C)
66	Yarrow	*Achillea millefolium*	-20°F (-29°C)

Cool-Season Tips

- **Seed-starting tips:**

  » **Seedling heat mat:** To provide warm but not hot conditions for starting most cool-season seeds, place a wire cooling rack on the seedling heat mat, then place the seeded trays on the rack. The air space between the rack and mat cools the mat and provides the consistent warmth the seeds need.

  » **Indoor growing space:** Warm soil and cool air temperatures (65 to 70°F [15.5 to 21°C]) are the best conditions for sprouting cool-season seeds.

  » See individual flower profiles for any additional specific tips on starting seeds.

- **Excellent drainage:** Planting in raised beds is recommended to provide the excellent drainage that this group prefers as cool outdoor temperatures can prolong wet conditions.

- **Row covers:** Protection from cold winter winds with lightweight row covers is beneficial.

- **Fall and winter plantings:** A sturdy, well-established transplant will fare best throughout winter.

- **Seed storage:** I store my cool-season seeds in the freezer to extend their viability and encourage strong germination once planted.

  » Place seed packets in an airtight container with a desiccant packet.

  » Leave the container at room temperature for 48 hours to allow the desiccant to absorb any moisture before moving it to the freezer.

  » Place in the freezer.

  » Remove the container from the freezer. Leave it at room temperature for 48 hours before opening to allow the desiccant to absorb any moisture as a result of thawing.

  » Seeds are ready to be planted.

ORLAYA

AGROSTEMMA

CARNATION

RUDBECKIA

SWEET WILLIAM

DIGITALIS

NIGELLA

NIGELLA

NIGELLA

Achillea millefolium

Yarrow

Yarrow is a gorgeous filler flower for bouquets and arrangements! The beneficial insects and the pollinators love it, too. The feathery green foliage is as lovely as the flat-topped clusters of tiny blooms, making this a "must grow" for gardeners and farmers alike.

Depending on your climate, you may be quite familiar with yarrow as a perennial that spreads far and wide, blanketing fields with yellow or pink blooms. However, there are hybrid versions of this plant introduced more recently that grow taller and offer a much broader range of flower colors. And these plants are not the spreaders that their wilder cousins tend to be.

The hybrid yarrow that is grown for cut flowers is considered a "short-lived perennial" and only seems to produce the best and most vibrant colors in the first season of growth. For that reason, we grow it as a cool-season hardy annual, planting each season in the fall for next summer's blooms. We've found that fall planting gets us the tallest stems possible. And even though we treat it as a cool-season hardy annual, we find that it also thrives in the heat, so it has a long harvest window.

home garden tip

Yarrow will continue to bloom throughout the summer if faded flowers are removed. weekly.

- **Seeding and growing tips:** Sow seeds on the surface of the ¾-inch (2 cm) soil blocks; do not cover. Keep the soil and seeds moist before germination; we cover trays with wide-weave burlap to help with this. The seedlings are ready to plant when 3 to 5 inches (7.5 to 13 cm) tall or wide—they may grow out more than up at first. Yarrow does well in lean soil, so after the standard bed preparation before planting, it shouldn't need additional fertilizer. In fact, too much fertilizer (specifically too much nitrogen) may result in all foliage and no flowers. Yarrow begins to flower with the longer day lengths (12 to 16 hours) of summer. Stems emerge from the plant base, so pinching is not required. Expect several stems per plant.

- **Flower support notes:** Support netting helps keep the thin stems and heavy,

growing facts

Preferred season: Cool

Winter low temperature: -20°F (-29°C)

Starting from seed:
- Prefer to start seed indoors
- Start seeds 4 to 6 weeks before planting outdoors
- Prefer to start in ¾-inch (2 cm) soil blocks
- Needs light to sprout; do not cover
- Soil temperature: 70°F (21°C)
- 7 to 14 days to sprout
- Air temperature for optimal transplant growth: 55 to 65°F (13 to 18°C)
- Transplant to the garden when: 3 to 5 inches (7.5 to 13 cm) tall

Sun requirement: Full sun

Height: 24–36 inches (60 to 90 cm)

Rows of plants per 36" (90 cm) wide bed: 4

Plant spacing in row: 6 inches (15 cm)

Days to bloom: 120–130

Flower support: Yes

Fertilization: Standard bed preparation (see page 57)

FROM FAR LEFT *Stage to harvest: To prevent wilting, harvest when the bloom only a few tiny flowers on the edge left to open.*

Transplant yarrow to the garden when the leaves reach 3 to 5 inches.

developing flower heads of the taller hybrid varieties upright during wind and rainstorms.

- **Harvesting and conditioning notes:** See Stage to harvest image (page 66). Harvest when all of the tiny blooms are open, otherwise wilting will occur. Harvesting in the coolest part of the day will also help prevent wilting—this can be either early morning or evening. Make the cut at or near ground level as additional stems will emerge from the base of the plant. Strip off side branches if they have immature (not fully open) blooms. Follow the standard conditioning steps on page 32. Yarrow is a member of the "Dirty Dozen Flowers" (see page 33 for details). It is thought to be somewhat ethylene sensitive. Expect fresh blooms to last 7 to 12 days in the vase, or hang blooms upside-down to dry.

- **Good to know:** Yarrow is deer resistant in my experience—another plus!

Favorite Varieties

'**Colorado Sunset**' is my go-to mix for its vast range of colors. We grow it to get those special shades of red, white, soft yellow, lavender, and shrimp that you don't normally see in the wild perennial varieties of yarrow; grows to 30 inches (75 cm) tall.

'**Summer Berries**' features bright colors including red, cerise, bright pinks, and some pastels; grows to 30 inches (75 cm) tall.

'**Summer Pastels**' flowers in soft pastel shades of lavender, purple, white, apricot, cream, rose, and pink; grows to 30 inches (75 cm) tall.

Left to right: Colorado Sunset and Summer Berries, both favorites

flower farmer insider tip

I usually do not grow mixes for production, as commercial customers prefer to purchase straight-color bunches. However, that is not the case with my favorite yarrows, which are only available as mixes. We find that different colors in these mixes may reach full bloom at slightly different rates, so even though we grow a color mix, we have the option of harvesting it either as single-color or mixed-color bunches. The soft light yellow and shrimp colors in the 'Colorado Sunset' are gorgeous and always in high demand.

Five-week-old Agrostemma seedlings whose seeds were planted in the garden.

Agrostemma githago
Corn Cockle

Corn cockle is one of the first flowers to bloom in spring here on my farm. It produces 1- to 2-inch (2.5 to 5 cm) blooms in a branching spray on each willowy stem. And although they look delicate, they hold up quite well as cut flowers, making a great spring filler flower. They're deer resistant for us, too, and look so beautiful dancing in the spring breeze.

Agrostemma is native to western Europe, so it prefers cool summers. That's certainly not a match for my summers, but I have had luck growing this as a cool-season hardy annual when planted in fall. It plays a role in my spring

bouquets similar to that of cosmos in my summer bouquets.

- **Seeding and growing tips:** As with my other fall direct-seeded flowers, I heavily seed in three rows per bed and then weed between those rows with my stand-up garden hoe several times in the fall. If this flower will not survive your winter temperatures, see my special note in "Planting Seeds in the Garden" (page 48). Fall-planted seedlings may benefit from additional fertilization in the field after the soil has warmed in spring and

growing facts

Preferred season: Cool

Winter low temperature: 10°F (-12°C)

Starting from seed:
- Prefer to sow directly in the garden
- Plant seeds 6 to 8 weeks before first fall frost
- Needs darkness to sprout; cover with soil
- Soil temperature: 60 to 70°F (15.5 to 21°C)
- 7 to 14 days to sprout

Sun requirement: Full sun, at least 6 to 8 hours

Height: 24–36 inches (60 to 90 cm)

Rows of plants per 36" (90 cm) wide bed: 3

Plant spacing in row: 4–6 inches (10–15 cm)

Days to bloom: 70–85

Flower support: Yes

Fertilization: Standard bed preparation (see page 57); additional field applications may be beneficial

home garden tip

Remove faded flowers regularly to encourage additional blooming, then, at the end of the season, allow a few flowers to mature and reseed the bed for next year.

new growth has started. In early spring when growth starts back up, I weed again and thin the rows to one plant every 4 to 6 inches (10 to 15 cm) or so. Pinching is not needed as the plant branches really well on its own; expect two to three stems per plant with a spray of multiple blooms on each stem. *Agrostemma* likes full sun, but, in warmer regions, it may benefit from some mid- to late-afternoon shade to extend bloom time a bit. In areas with cool summers, it might be possible to plant a succession in spring to prolong the season.

- **Flower support notes:** This flower benefits from support netting; the willowy branching stems can become very tangled as they sway in the breeze.

- **Harvesting and conditioning notes:** See Stage to harvest image (page 71). Harvest when the first blooms on the spray just begin to crack open. Any open blooms may get damaged and discolored from rain, so watch the weather. Flowers continue to open after cutting. Because they can get very tangled, I cut these a little bit differently—I grab several at a time and make the cut at ground level, then pull them down through the support netting. I strip the bottom two-thirds of the stem and either keep them all together as a big spray of blooms and rubber band the bunches in the garden, or cut them down to several smaller stems to suit our use. To prevent wilting, cut in the coolest part of the day, and remove the lower foliage. Follow the standard conditioning steps on page 32. This flower benefits from the use of holding solution and is not known to be ethylene sensitive. With proper water conditioning, expect fresh blooms to last 5 to 7 days in the vase.

flower farmer insider tip

In my experience, these flowers were more popular at markets than with florists. This flower in straight bunches, displayed at the front of my farmers' market booth, caused a stir and even drew in nonflower people! Leaving the stems long and placing the buckets at eye level was very captivating.

- Good to know: All parts of this plant, including the seeds, are considered poisonous. Please use caution around pets, livestock, and children.

Favorite Varieties

'Ocean Pearl' is the all-white variety with lovely veining on the petals that looks like it was painted or drawn on. Bugs particularly love white flowers, so you may need to harvest this one earlier than the other to avoid bug damage; grows 24 to 36 inches (60 to 90 cm) tall.

'Purple Queen' is white in the flower's center, then gradually deepens to purple from the middle of the petal and out toward the tip; grows 24 to 36 inches (60 to 90 cm) tall.

Stage to harvest: This multi-bloom per stem flower I like to harvest with 25% or so open and the rest in bud that quickly open after harvest.

This flower appears delicate but has a good vase life. A mix of 'Ocean Pearls' and 'Purple Queen.'

Ammobium alatum

Winged Everlasting

The common name "winged everlasting" is a great description of this lovely plant. "Winged" refers to the winged shape of the stems (similar to statice in that way), and "everlasting" refers to how wonderfully it dries.

This plant is like a combination of two of my favorites: I get a flower that looks similar to feverfew, and it's easy to dry like statice. I'm in heaven, and I'm not alone! Florists also love using *Ammobium* in both their fresh and dried designs, especially for boutonnieres and corsages, and it's great for crafting as well.

This flower's white outer "petals" are actually papery bracts, with a little yellow floret inside. They are typically harvested for cut flowers before they are fully open, but in a garden setting, once fully open the yellow centers attract small pollinators and beneficial insects.

Transplant when the leaves reach 3 to 5 inches long.

home garden tip

These flowers are fun to grow in borders, rocky or sandy areas, roadsides, and the like. As the flowers dry on the plant, they are still visually interesting going into fall and winter. For true "everlasting" flowers, cut some and hang them indoors to dry.

Ammobium is native to Australia, where it is known as a tender perennial and can be found growing along roadsides and in disturbed areas such as empty fields. However, in most other places it is grown as a cool-season hardy annual. In my area, I've found it can also be fall planted with row cover protection.

- **Seeding and growing tips:** I'm able to fall plant these with row cover protection, but in places with colder winters, plant them in early spring with row cover protection. I sow these in ¾-inch (2 cm) soil blocks covered only very lightly with soil. I do this by pushing the seed deeper into the soil block, which creates darkness. They're ready to transplant when 3 to 5 inches (7.5 to 13 cm) tall or wide; this plant grows wide instead of tall until flower stems start to emerge. The plants require very well-draining soil with ample fertilization—consider adding a balanced liquid fertilizer monthly in the field or garden. Stems emerge from the plant base and branch well on their own, so pinching is

growing facts

Preferred season: Cool

Winter low temperature: 20°F (-7°C)

Starting from seed:

- Prefer to start seed indoors
- Start seeds 4 to 6 weeks before planting outdoors
- Prefer to start in ¾-inch (2 cm) soil blocks
- Needs darkness to sprout; cover very lightly with soil
- Soil temperature: 65 to 70°F (18 to 21°C)
- 4 to 8 days to sprout
- Air temperature for optimal transplant growth: 65 to 70°F (18 to 21°C)
- Transplant to the garden when: 3 to 5 inches (7.5 to 13 cm) tall or wide

Sun requirement: Full sun

Height: 24–36 inches (50 to 66 cm)

Rows of plants per 36" (90 cm) wide bed: 4

Plant spacing in row: 6 inches (15 cm)

Days to bloom: 70–80

Flower support: Yes

Fertilization: Standard bed preparation (see page 57)

Fall and early spring planting grow abundance and excellent stem length. Nice spring bouquet filler and is a good dried flower.

not required. Expect multiple stems per plant until the first frost in fall.

- **Flower support notes:** This flower should be netted to keep it upright and straight in the garden. It quickly goes down in rainstorms.

- **Harvesting and conditioning notes:** See Stage to harvest image (page 74). For the cleanest and best quality fresh and dried flowers, harvest when the white bracts are not yet completely open and before the yellow center is visible. Flowers continue to open after cutting. Making the cut at ground level, additional stems emerge from the base. They don't have a lot of foliage, just a little at the bottom that should be stripped off. Follow the standard conditioning steps on page 32. Because of the stem's shape, fresh *Ammobium* stems can harbor bacteria, so they benefit from water conditioning treatments (CVBN tablets, holding solution, and flower food). *Ammobium* is not known to be ethylene sensitive. Expect fresh blooms to last 10 to 14 days in the vase, or indefinitely if dried.

Stage to harvest: A multi-flower per stem and I cut when the center first flower shows yellow.

- **Good to know:** There do not appear to be any hybrids offered that are specifically for cut-flower production (yet), so all seeds listed under this name should be the same heirloom variety.

flower farmer insider tip

Because this is such a versatile plant with a relatively short number of days to maturity, I recommend tests with succession planting. Anything you don't sell fresh should be cut and dried.

Favorite Varieties

'Grandiflorum' has bright green clumps of leaves that form a base rosette. Several winged and multibranched flower stems emerge, each with clusters of delicate, less-than-1-inch (2.5 cm) papery white blooms at the top with bright yellow floret centers; grows 20 to 30 inches (50 to 75 cm) tall.

Antirrhinum majus

Snapdragon

I've held snaps near and dear since my start as a flower farmer. Because snaps are such a significant cut-flower crop, I tackled starting them from seed as my very first seed using soil blocks. I remember that morning of discovering those first newborn baby snap seedlings—pure joy. After several dreadful seed-starting failures using other methods, this success was just the push I needed to start my flower-growing business.

My personal connection with snaps and their important role in the flower world was further affirmed during a vendor interview with Libbey Oliver, market manager of the Williamsburg Farmers Market. Libbey is a well-known flower arranger, author, and past manager of flower services at Colonial Williamsburg. She came to inspect my flower farm and, when she stepped into my workshop full of buckets of flowers, she stopped dead in her tracks, closed her eyes, took in a deep breath to embrace the aroma, and said, "Ah, I smell wonderful garden snaps!" Her reaction to the fragrance of my snapdragons, fresh from the garden, was the encouragement I needed to keep going.

I grow several varieties of snaps and follow a simple method of planting and growing them outdoors in my garden. I recommend that home gardeners and flower farmers start and follow along with what has become my go-to plan to get an easy start with this hardy flower. Once

Snap transplants that were 3 to 5 inches tall when planted 4 weeks before this picture, then pinched 14 days after planting.

ABOVE, FROM TOP *Madame Butterfly have double blooms that are not like any other snapdragon, plus the colors are really rich like ivory, rose, and bronze-white.*

Chantilly snaps are the first to bloom in spring in my garden and have open faced blooms so another different look plus the colors are unique.

you experience successful harvests, explore the steps to extend the season as described in Flower Farmer Insider Tip (see page 74).

If snaps survive your lowest winter temperatures, plant transplants in fall. These well-established plants reward with more stems, long stems, and excellent disease resistance. I plant all those varieties listed in my favorites at the same time in fall. Their blooming time is naturally varied in spring as their preferred day length conditions occur according to their groups, which are defined in the tips box.

If snaps do not survive your winter's lowest temperatures, plant transplants in very early spring. When selecting varieties for early spring planting, keep in mind that those in groups 1 and 2 that bloom during shorter day lengths and cooler conditions may not have enough growing time to get good stem length before blooming. If you have long, cool spring conditions, this may not be an issue. If your growing conditions tend to go straight from winter conditions quickly into summer heat, focus on varieties from groups 3 and 4 for best results. Experimenting with variety selection is the best way to find the best choices for your growing conditions.

home garden tip

'TGW Dragons' seed mixes are a great way to get many different snapdragon varieties planted in a small space and have these flowers blooming throughout their natural season. Snapdragons can also be grown in containers and look lovely in mixed plantings. Keep spent flower stalks cut to encourage additional blooms. Snaps are a favorite of the bees and hummingbirds, too.

'TGW Dragon Pink' includes up to 13 different shades and varieties that provide a wider window of bloom with one planting.

growing facts

Preferred season: Cool

Winter low temperature: 0°F (-18°C)

Starting from seed:

- Prefer to start seed indoors
- Start seed indoors 4 to 6 weeks before planting outdoors
- Prefer to start in ¾-inch (2 cm) soil blocks
- Needs light to sprout; do not cover
- Soil temperature: 70°F (21°C)
- 3 to 7 days to sprout
- Air temperature for optimal transplant growth: 60°F (15.5°C)
- Transplant to the garden when: 3 to 5 inches (7.5 to 13 cm) tall

Sun requirement: Minimum 8 hours, more is better

Height: 24–36 inches (50 to 66 cm)

Rows of plants per 36" (90 cm) wide bed: 4

Plant spacing in row: 6 inches (15 cm)

Days to bloom: roughly 90 days, depending on variety and season

Flower support: Yes

Fertilization: Standard bed preparation (see page 57); additional field applications are beneficial

- **Seeding and growing tips:** Sow seeds firmly on the surface of the soil blocks. Newly sown seeds need to be kept moist, so I lay wide-weave burlap over the blocks until the seeds start to crack. Sometimes after sprouting, the seed casing doesn't want to come off, which can make it look like your seedlings have no leaves. In that case, spritz the newborn seedlings with water to loosen them so they'll fall off. All varieties can be pinched to encourage branching and may result in an additional four to six blooms per plant. See "Pinching Plants" (page 53). If growing as unpinched transplants for large single blooms, spacing is 8 to 12 plants per square foot. To minimize disease issues, water with drip irrigation, or at the base of individual plants, rather than overhead.

- **Flower support notes:** Snapdragons must be netted to keep the stems straight. This is because they are both phototropic (bending toward light sources) and geotropic (bending to grow against gravity). If they are allowed to lay over from winds or a storm, the stems will immediately bend toward the sky and cannot be straightened again. Install netting at the halfway mark of the mature plant's height before plants reach that height.

ABOVE, FROM TOP *Stage to harvest: Cut when the first bottom flower is opening to prevent premature bloom drop from bee pollination. With the proper conditioning steps, stems continue to develop and open beautifully indoors.*

A cafeteria tray of 240 four-week-old snapdragons, 3-5" tall, growing in the ¾" soil blocks ready to transplant to the garden.

- **Harvesting and conditioning notes:** See Stage to harvest image at left. Snapdragon flowers open from bottom to top on the stalk. I harvest when the first bottom flower opens, as the other flowers on the stalk will continue to open after cutting. Make the first cut of the central stem almost at ground level, just above the lowest two to three leaves. Any future cuts should be made at the stem base. Strip off most of the leaves. Harvest into tall, narrow buckets that you can fill so the stems stay upright and straight. As with most spike-shaped flowers, snapdragons are ethylene sensitive. Snaps benefit from chlorine tabs in the harvest container, holding solution in storage, as well as flower food in the vase so flowers continue to open and retain their color. With proper conditioning, expect flowers to last 7 to 9 days in the vase.

- **Good to know:** Once a flower has been pollinated, it will quickly shrivel and fall off as the seed starts to form. This is why you may see some stalks with blooms falling off at the bottom but closed flowers still at the top. If you have lots of pollinators in your area, cut your snapdragons earlier to avoid this issue.

flower farmer insider tip

Succession planting is highly recommended, utilizing plants from different groups as the seasons progress. For commercial sales, snapdragons are not typically pinched, as the longer center stems sell for a higher price. To grow them as single-stem plants, sow up to three seeds per ¾-inch (2 cm) soil block, then transplant those blocks, one per 6 × 6-inch (15 × 15 cm) space.

Favorite Varieties

'Chantilly' tends to be the first to bloom and first to finish as spring starts to heat up. The open-face blooms are in unique shades of peach, pink, yellow, and white and grow 24 to 36 inches (60 to 90 cm) tall.

'Madame Butterfly' features ruffle-edged double blooms that florists often can't get from the wholesaler. It blooms in red, white, rose, yellow, and pink and grows 24 to 36 inches (60 to 90 cm) tall.

'Opus' features beautiful bicolor blooms. A productive and long-blooming flower with sturdy stems that blooms into summer. This traditional bloom shape includes colors such as apple blossom, fresh white, bronze, yellow, red, lavender, and pink, growing 24 to 36 inches (60 to 90 cm) tall.

'Potomac' is an excellent variety for warm temperatures, long days, and the strong light conditions of summer. It blooms in colors of white, yellow, apple blossom, cherry rose, royal, orange, pink, and lavender. The tallest one I grow here typically reaches 40 to 60 inches (100 to 150 cm).

'Rocket' is one of the latest varieties to bloom in my garden from fall planting. Its colors include white, yellow, pink, lipstick, and magenta and the plant grows 24 to 40 inches (60 to 100 cm) tall.

'TGW Dragons' is a custom seed mix created and sold by The Gardener's Workshop. Mixes are available in pink, yellow, white, and sunset; plants grow 24 to 40 inches (60 to 100 cm) tall.

flower farmer insider tip with
Dave Dowling, Cut-Flower Specialist with Ball Seed

"In catalog descriptions for snapdragons, you may see a number that indicates which group the flower is in. The different groups indicate when the variety will bloom (not when to plant them) and the level of heat and day length it prefers."

Groups 1 and 2: Bloom during late winter and early spring, during short days and cool temperatures.
- The earliest snap varieties bloom in the garden in spring.
- Where winters temperatures don't go below freezing, or in a temperature- and light-controlled greenhouse, these groups blooms in late winter and early spring.
- Variety examples: 'Chantilly' and 'Maryland'

Group 3: Blooms in either late spring or fall, depending on planting date.
- In the garden, this group blooms late spring to early summer, when planted in fall or very early spring.
- For fall blooming, plant in late summer about 100 days before the first expected frost.
- Example: 'Madame Butterfly'

Group 4: Blooms in summer with the longest day lengths and warmest temperatures.
- This is the latest-blooming group in the garden when planted in fall or early spring.
- These are the best candidates for summer succession plantings until mid-June.
- Examples: 'Rocket', 'Potomac', 'Opus'

Brassica oleracea

Ornamental Cabbage, Ornamental Kale, Flowering Kale

Growing flowering kale is a fun way to extend your flower season! Bitter to the taste, these hybrid varieties of kale were specifically developed for cut-flower ornamental use, with their rose-like leaf growth pattern and lovely center colors. They can even have bicolor centers and may have smooth, ruffled, or feathery leaves. They're deer resistant, which is great news!

For many years, I found myself too busy harvesting and selling summer flowers to get ornamental kale seed started at the proper time. But once I committed to starting the seeds mid-summer, indoors in an air-conditioned space, what a rewarding fall crop I reaped!

- **Seeding and growing tips:** Sow three seeds per plug tray cell or soil block for speedier planting. Do not thin these seedling clusters. Seedlings prefer to grow cool, in about 60°F (15.5°C) air temperatures. Plant four rows in the bed, with the seedling clusters 6 inches

home garden tip

Ornamental kale looks great displayed alongside fall mums, broom corn, ornamental grasses, pumpkins, and gourds.

Beautiful kale varieties grown on Wind Haven Flower Farm. From left to right: 'Feather King,' 'Feather Queen', 'Flare Rose', 'Lucir White', 'First Lady', 'Crane Pink', 'Crane White', 'Sunset', and 'Flare White'.

(15 cm) apart in the row. This will encourage the desired smaller 3- to 6-inch (7.5 to 15 cm) head size and prevent the stems from growing too thick to use as cut flowers. Kale likes moist but well-drained soil, so a raised bed with drip irrigation is ideal. Each plant produces a single stem. We find these get the same attention from cabbage moths as the rest of this plant family. To prevent damage, I like to cover the planting with lightweight row covers immediately after planting to prevent the moths' access to the plants to lay their eggs, or you can treat the plants with Bt (*Bacillus thuringiensis*), an organic treatment that targets only those caterpillars that eat the plant leaves. Field applications of fertilizer may be beneficial, but discontinue that once the plants start to color up, which they will do once nighttime temperatures go below 50°F (10°C). They tolerate light frost but should be harvested before a hard freeze or heavy snowfall.

- **Flower support notes:** Install flower support netting soon after planting to encourage the plants to grow straight up and to keep top-heavy heads upright.

- **Harvesting and conditioning notes:** See Stage to harvest image (page 82). Harvest when the leaves are mature and the rosettes have colored up nicely. Make the cut at or near ground level, or however long you need the stem to be. The more leaves you strip, the smaller the head becomes. Follow the standard conditioning steps on page 32. These plants benefit from holding solution, and regular water changes can help avoid unpleasant odors that sometimes develop as the cut stems age. Ornamental kale is not known to be ethylene sensitive. Expect fresh blooms to last 5 to 10 days in the vase.

growing facts

Preferred season: Cool

Winter low temperature: 10°F (-12°C)

Starting from seed:
- Prefer to start seed indoors
- Start seeds 4 to 6 weeks before planting outdoors
- Prefer to start in 128-cell plug trays or 2-inch (5 cm) soil blocks
- Prefers light to sprout; do not cover
- Soil temperature: 70°F (21°C)
- 10 to 14 days to sprout
- Air temperature for optimal transplant growth: 60°F (15.5°C)
- Transplant to the garden when: 3 to 5 inches (7.5 to 13 cm) tall

Sun requirement: Full sun, part shade

Height: 24–36 inches (60 to 90 cm)

Rows of plants per 36" (90 cm) wide bed: 4 seedling clusters (see Tips)

Plant spacing in row: 6 inches (15 cm) or less

Days to bloom: 90 to 110

Flower support: Yes

Fertilization: Standard bed preparation (see page 57); additional field applications may be beneficial

flower farmer insider tip

This plant is an in-demand florist crop and fun for the late-season farmers' market! Be thinking about what other flowers you'll have to sell at this time (late fall) and choose colors that coordinate. Florists like the heads to be in the 6-inch (15 cm) or smaller range.

- **Good to know:** There are some varieties of ornamental kale that are meant to be used as bedding plants or in containers; these do not get tall enough to be used as cut flowers. If you intend to grow them as cut flowers, make sure the variety you choose is expected to grow at least 24 inches (60 cm) tall.

Favorite Varieties

'**Crane**' is a variety commonly grown by cut-flower growers, offering center colors in a creamy white, white/pink bicolor, pink, rose, and red (actually more of a purplish magenta). The outer leaves may be ruffled and have veining that matches the center color; grows 24 to 36 inches (60 to 90 cm) tall.

LEFT FROM TOP *Stage to harvest: Color intensifies after a fall frost. Harvest anytime there is enough length and head size. Remove more leaves up the stem to reduce overall size.*

I sowed 3 to 4 seeds per Swift Blocker 27; they are planted as a cluster to help reduce stem thickness and to grow taller. Plant when 3 to 5 inches tall.

Bupleurum rotundifolium

Bupleurum, Hare's Ear, Hound's Ear

Bupleurum has a unique look and color, with its clusters of tiny yellow-green flowers, angular branching, and cupped leaves that appear to have stems growing right up through them. Bupleurum is great as a green filler for bouquets, adding interest and height to spring bouquets. We could never grow enough to meet demand. An added benefit of having bupleurum in my garden is that it attracts spring pollinators and provides much-needed moisture for beneficial insects by holding rainwater drops in its cupped leaves. It is also deer resistant and a good reseeder in the landscape or garden.

Stage to harvest: Bupleurum has a wide window of harvest, any time after most of the tiny flowers have opened until it is developing a seed head.

growing facts

Preferred season: Cool

Winter low temperature survival: -10°F (-23°C)

Starting from seed:

- Prefer to sow directly in the field or garden
- Plant seeds 6 to 8 weeks before first fall frost
- Needs darkness to sprout; cover with soil
- Soil temperature: 55°F (13°C)
- 10 to 21 days to sprout
- Air temperature for optimal growth: 60 to 65°F (15.5 to 18°C)

Sun requirement: Full sun, minimum 6 to 8 hours

Height: 24 to 48 inches (60 to 120 cm)

Rows of plants per 36-inch (90 cm)-wide bed: 3

Plant spacing in row: 6 inches (15 cm)

Days to bloom: 80 to 90

Flower support: Yes

Fertilization: Standard bed preparation (see page 57); additional field applications may be beneficial

home garden tip

Left to develop in the garden or landscape, these flowers are beautiful for several weeks, eventually developing lovely seed heads.

- **Seeding and growing tips:** It is helpful to store seeds for at least 2 weeks in the freezer before planting for the best germination. We direct seed in the garden in fall. If this flower will not survive your winter temperatures, see my special note in "Planting Seeds in the Garden" (page 48), and my tips following for starting indoors.

  Sown in the garden, bupleurum can be slow to sprout and, when it does, the tiny, dark seedlings have thin foliage, making them hard to see. Fall-planted seedlings may benefit from additional fertilization in the field after the soil has warmed in spring and new growth has restarted. Once the seedlings are about 5 inches (13 cm) tall in spring, thin them to about one every 6 inches (15 cm) or so for cut flowers. I tend to treat this as a flash crop, leaving the plants spaced more closely together because I only harvest one main stem per plant.

- **Flower support notes:** I use flower support netting.

- **Harvesting and conditioning notes:** See Stage to harvest image (page 83). Harvesting can begin when flowers show color and continue all through the lifecycle up to seed head development. Harvesting very early may result in wilting flowers, so experiment until you find the earliest you can cut in your environmental conditions. Flowers continue to open after cutting. Harvest the center stem just above the bottom two or three side shoots and experiment with side shoot growth in your climate. This plant is not ethylene sensitive. Follow the standard conditioning steps on page 32. The flowers benefit from hydrating overnight before arranging.

With proper conditioning, expect them to last 7 days in the vase.

- **Good to know:** Bupleurum dries beautifully!

Favorite Varieties

'Green Gold' features 2½-inch (6 cm) yellow–lime green flower clusters atop long, wiry stems. Excellent for mixed bouquets; grows 24 to 48 inches (60 to 120 cm) tall.

LEFT, FROM TOP, *Seeds planted in the garden from just sprouted after 10 days in cool conditions to several weeks old.*

Notice how thin and tiny the newly emerging seedlings are that make them easy to overlook.

A sought-after filler for its light and airy stems of tiny flowers. I've never had enough.

flower farmer insider tip

I succession plant bupleurum. My most abundant and tallest crop is directly sown in fall when I cannot provide cool enough conditions indoors to get it to sprout. But once temperatures cool naturally in winter, I start seed indoors in plug trays, placing them in a cool to cold space like a garage or the floor of a greenhouse. I sow seeds into 128-cell plug trays filled with moistened potting mix. In each cell, sow two or three seeds on the surface, pushing them down with your finger.

Do not cover the seeds with soil as you would when planting seeds outdoors. Place a second empty cell tray, upside-down, over the filled tray to create the required darkness but still allow plenty of oxygen to reach the seed by not covering it with soil. Place the trays in a cool spot and leave them there for 10 to 14 days. Water as needed. Once 50 percent of the seedlings sprout, remove the top tray and place the seedlings under a grow light until they reach the recommended 3 to 5 inches (7.5 to 13 cm) tall for planting. I do not thin, but transplant the clusters into a bed 6 inches (15 cm) apart in four rows. I start seeds weekly up to 8 weeks or so before the heat of summer starts.

Calendula officinalis
Pot marigold

Pot marigolds are not to be confused with marigolds, though they have similar common names. Although calendula has been cultivated since ancient times as a medicinal plant and a natural dye, it's also a fantastic ornamental and pollinator plant, whether grown in a garden, a container, or in the field for cutting.

Calendula is always one of the first bloomers on my farm, and so we've nicknamed it "spring zinnia" because of its bright colors and disk flower shape. Except in the warmest climates where it can perennialize, calendula is considered a cool-season hardy annual plant, and that is how we grow it. We get the longest stems by planting them in fall and protecting them with row cover during winter.

Historically available as a beautiful golden-orange flower, hybrid varieties have come to market that offer additional colors, such as yellow, ivory, pink, and red.

home garden tip

If kept free of faded flowers, calendula will continue to bloom until the first frost. Leave a few flowers to mature at the end of the season to reseed for next year.

- **Seeding and growing tips:** We start calendula indoors in 2-inch (5 cm) soil blocks or 128-cell plug trays due to the large seed size. Fall planting is ideal for the best stem length, but if it will not survive winter temperatures in your area, plant in very early spring and protect with row cover. To extend blooming in warmer climates, consider planting where it will get afternoon shade. No fertilization is needed beyond standard bed preparation. The plant produces many stems from the base, so pinching is not required.

- **Flower support notes:** The base of this plant is low-growing, but the taller flower stems benefit from support, particularly in wind and rain storms.

- **Harvesting and conditioning notes:** See Stage to harvest image (page 88). Harvest when flowers just begin to crack open, making the cut at ground level. Use gloves to harvest as the stems and foliage may have a sticky residue. Strip most of the foliage. Follow the standard conditioning steps on page 32. Pot marigold is a member of the "Dirty Dozen Flowers" (see page 33 for details). Calendula is not ethylene sensitive. If properly conditioned, expect fresh blooms to last 5 to 7 days in the vase. They can also be hung in bunches to dry, or blooms can be cut from stems and dried flat to use in decor or craft projects.

- **Good to know:** Calendula petals are edible and are commonly used to accent salads, rice dishes, soups, and desserts.

growing facts

Preferred season: Cool

Winter low temperature survival: 10°F (-12°C)

Starting from seed:
- Prefer to start seed indoors
- Start seed indoors 4 weeks before planting outdoors
- Prefer to start in 2-inch (5 cm) soil blocks or 128-cell plug tray
- Needs darkness to sprout; cover with soil to ½ inch (1 cm)
- Soil temperature: 70°F (21°C)
- 10 to 14 days to sprout
- Air temperature for optimal transplant growth: 70°F (21°C)
- Transplant to the garden when: 3 to 5 inches (7.5 to 13 cm) tall

Sun requirement: Full sun, partial shade (4 to 8 hours)

Height: 12 to 24 inches (30 to 60 cm)

Rows of plants per 36-inch (90 cm)-wide bed: 4

Plant spacing in row: 6 inches (15 cm)

Days to bloom: 50 to 60

Flower support: Yes

Fertilization: Standard bed preparation (see page 57)

FROM FAR LEFT *The bloom progression of Greenheart Orange. I love its hard fleshy green center that pops the orange petals.*

Calendula seedlings are transplanted when their leaves reach 3 to 5 inches long.

Favorite Varieties

'Cantaloupe' blooms come in mixed colors including apricot, cream, and pink. The flower centers are dark or yellow; they make a lovely bouquet all by themselves; grows to 24 inches (60 cm) tall.

'Greenheart Orange' is a larger, 3-inch (7.5 cm), bright-orange double bloom with an unusual textured green center. A very unique-looking flower! Orange is my favorite color, and this one does not disappoint; grows to 24 inches (60 cm) tall.

'Ivory Princess' is a sort of buttery cream and gold with a brown center. Produces 2- to 3-inch (5 to 7.5 cm) double and semidouble blooms. This is a good one to coordinate with softer palettes; grows to 24 inches (60 cm) tall.

flower farmer insider tip

Calendula may not be a good crop for all farms. It is a fast, early spring grower with a stem length on the shorter end of the cut-flower spectrum. Consider whether you can have other flowers blooming at this time of year to make bouquets with, and even more important, whether you have a way to sell flowers so early in the season. In my garden, this flower blooms alongside Iceland poppy and bachelor button. It pairs beautifully with dill foliage.

'Pacific Beauties' is a nice mix of large double apricot, orange, gold, cream, and yellow blooms; grows to 24 inches (60 cm) tall.

Left to right: 'Ivory Princess', 'Pacific Beauties Mix', 'Cantaloupe Mix', and Stage to harvest.

Campanula medium

Canterbury Bells, Bellflower, Cup and Saucer

These large, showy blooms look fantastic alongside other spring beauties such as larkspur and foxglove, both in the garden and in mixed bouquets. I absolutely love that the open flowers hold water after rain for the pollinators and beneficial insects to enjoy.

You may be familiar with varieties of bellflower that are perennial in your region. Those perennial varieties require about 12 weeks of colder weather (under 40°F [4°C]) in winter to bloom the following year. At my farm, I just can't count on that happening. So, the varieties of campanula that I grow are designed specifically

home garden tip

To support these top-heavy blooms, you may choose to use the more decorative metal support grids like those used for peonies, rather than the white plastic support netting I use in the field.

3 to 5-inch transplants are ready for planting. Campanula can be challenging to provide their required germination conditions, so I most often order plugs to arrive in fall. See Resources on page 230.

growing facts

Preferred season: Cool

Winter low temperature survival: -10°F (-23°C)

Starting from seed:
- Prefer to start seed indoors
- Start seeds 6 to 8 weeks before planting outdoors
- Prefer to start in ¾-inch (2 cm) soil blocks
- Needs light to sprout; do not cover
- Soil temperature: 65 to 68°F (18 to 20°C)
- 14 to 21 days to sprout
- Air temperature for optimal transplant growth: 55 to 60°F (13 to 15.5°C)
- Transplant to the garden when: 3 to 5 inches (7.5 to 13 cm) tall

Sun requirement: At least 6 to 8 hours of sun; tolerates part shade

Height: 24 to 48 inches (60 to 120 cm)

Rows of plants per 36-inch (90 cm)-wide bed: 4

Plant spacing in row: 6 inches (15 cm)

Days to bloom: 120 to 140

Flower support: Yes

Fertilization: Standard bed preparation (see page 57); additional field applications may be beneficial

for growing as an annual plant, one that blooms in the first year of growth and produces beautiful, more upright blooms for use as cut flowers; they are extremely winter hardy.

- **Seeding and growing tips:** To thrive, campanula needs to live as a young transplant in the garden during cooler, shorter days (less than 12 hours of daylight) to develop foliage and stem length, then have longer (but still cool) days after that to initiate flowering. I find that fall-planted seedlings produce the tallest stems, so I plant in fall. Sow seeds firmly on the surface of ¾-inch (2 cm) soil blocks. Campanula transplants must be kept in cool temperatures, definitely lower than 72°F (22°C) at night and 82°F (28°C) during the day, to prevent rosetting. Campanula develops a taproot, so to avoid transplant shock, plant outside when they have two or three true leaves. Campanula benefits from an application of balanced fertilizer in the field in spring after the soil has warmed and new growth is visible. Expect several stems per plant. Pinching is not required but can be done and may result in larger and more usable side shoots. Rather than doing that, though, I make a deep first cut on the center stem. If pinching in the garden bed, plant 9 inches (23 cm) apart. If not pinching (to harvest large single stems), plant 4 to 6 inches (10 to 15 cm) apart.

- **Flower support notes:** Flower support netting is mandatory to keep these heavy blooms upright.

- **Harvesting and conditioning notes:** See Stage to harvest image (page 91). Harvest when the first two or three bells on a stem begin to open. Make the cut almost at ground level, just above the first two or three side shoots. Future cuts can be made at the base of the stem. I strip the bottom half of the stem. Follow the standard conditioning steps on page 32. Cut stems benefit from the use of holding solution and flower food to

ABOVE, FROM LEFT *Stage to harvest: Cut the stem as the first blooms are opening to help prevent weather damage.*

A big, beautiful bunch of 'Champion II' in lilac. Lighter colors don't show rain damage as much as darker colors.

flower farmer insider tip

Because these plants have a longer growth period and specific seedling temperature requirements, it may be more dependable to order campanula as plugs to plant out in fall, rather than starting them from seed.

help blooms continue to open and color up. Campanula is very ethylene sensitive. With proper conditioning, expect fresh blooms to last 7 to 14 days in the vase.

- **Good to know:** The deer seem very attracted to these on our property, so we spread row cover over them as soon as they're planted to make sure the deer don't discover them. I sometimes use deer-repellant sprays also.

Favorite Varieties

'Champion' includes several in the series: 'Champion', 'Champion II', and 'Champion Pro'. They are all similar in look and make great cut flowers. The most recent introduction, 'Champion Pro', is a fast grower that produces more stems than other 'Champion' varieties. Its blooms are slightly smaller, but there are more per stem. They bloom in lavender, white, pink, and deep blue; grows 24 to 48 inches (60 to 120 cm) tall.

Centaurea cyanus

Bachelor Button, Cornflower

Bachelor buttons are great flowers to grow whether you intend to harvest for cut flowers or not. They are always one of the very first spring bloomers on my farm, but even before they bloom, they're producing nectar (excreted through the leaves) to attract beneficial bugs to my garden for the season. They have such distinctive silvery foliage and stems! And although the classic blue flower is most common, the pink, white, and purple varieties are equally lovely, particularly when planted mixed together. They are also deer resistant, which is always a plus!

home garden tip

At the end of their season, leave a few flowers to mature and reseed the garden for next year.

- **Seeding and growing tips:** For me, the key to getting a good stand of bachelor button has been a heavily seeded fall planting that we don't thin until early spring. If they survive your winter temperatures, I urge you to do the same. Even if you're on the cusp, consider fall planting them with a lightweight row cover. If this flower will not survive your winter temperatures, see my special note in "Planting Seeds in the Garden" (page 48). I do not use mulch film on direct-seeded beds. Instead, I plant three rows per bed because this gives me the space needed to run my hoe through to weed quickly, which I do several times in the fall. Fall-planted seedlings may benefit especially from additional fertilization in the field after the soil has warmed in spring and new growth has started. In early spring, when growth starts back up, I weed again and thin

the rows to one plant every 6 inches (15 cm) or so. Bachelor button requires full sun and begins to bloom as days lengthen moving toward summer solstice.

- **Flower support notes:** This flower will benefit from support netting to protect from rain and windstorms.

- **Harvesting and conditioning notes:** See Stage to harvest image below. To use as a fresh-cut flower, cut when color begins to show on the top of the bud. To use for drying, cut when the blooms are open. Flowers continue to open after cutting. Harvest the central stem almost at ground level, just above the lowest three or four side shoots. Future harvests can be made at the base of the stem. For best hydration, strip off all lower leaves and branches. Follow the standard conditioning steps on page 32. Bachelor button is a member of the "Dirty Dozen Flowers" (see page 33 for details). This flower is known to be ethylene sensitive.

growing facts

Preferred season: Cool

Winter low temperature survival: 0°F (-18°C)

Starting from seed:
- Prefer to sow directly in the field or garden
- Plant seeds 6 to 8 weeks before first fall frost
- Needs darkness to sprout; plant ¼ inch (0.6 cm) deep
- Soil temperature: 65 to 75°F (18 to 24°C)
- 7 to 14 days to sprout

Sun requirement: Full sun

Height: 24 to 36 inches (60 to 90 cm)

Rows of plants per 36-inch (90 cm)-wide bed: 3

Plant spacing in row: 6 inches (15 cm)

Days to bloom: 65 to 75 days

Flower support: Yes

Fertilization: Standard bed preparation (see page 57); additional field applications may be beneficial

FROM FAR LEFT *Seeds planted in the garden from just sprouting to several weeks old.*

Stage to harvest: To help intensify the colors, harvest at just-cracking-open stage and allow blooms to open indoors out of wind and hot sun.

93

flower farmer insider tip

This flower is not very big and can be challenging to learn to harvest—but on the plus side, it comes in true blue and is an early bloomer. I found that growing just a small portion produced enough to add a beautiful pop to our spring bouquets and made it possible for me to keep up with the harvest, which extended it well to the start of summer. Florists tend to prefer solid colors for arranging, and especially that striking classic blue that is otherwise so hard to come by in the flower world.

With proper water conditioning, expect fresh blooms to last 7 to 10 days in the vase. Flowers dry well but shrink considerably.

- **Good to know:** The petals are edible and are commonly used to garnish cold drinks, desserts, and salads. Do not eat flowers that have been treated with cut-flower conditioning chemicals.

Favorite Varieties

'Boy series', in both the traditional blue and pink colors, is what we grow as a cut flower for florists and bouquets, and the 'Mix' is grown for garden, landscape, or container plantings. Colors include solids, such as white, black, blue, pink, and purple blooms; grows to 36 inches (90 cm) tall.

'Classic series' offers beautiful semidouble and double blooms in color mixes that we just love! We grow 'Romantic' (pink and white with bicolor), 'Magic' (purple and white with bicolor), and 'Fantastic' (blue and white with bicolor); grows to 36 inches (90 cm) tall.

Left bucket from the top: 'Classic Magic', 'Classic Fantastic', and 'Classic Romance'. Right bucket: 'Boy Blue' and 'Boy Pinkie'.

Cerinthe major

Honeywort

Cerinthe is a flower I've fallen in love with recently, and with good reason. I just had to learn how to get those stems tall enough! And as with so many of these cool-season hardy annuals, *Cerinthe* needs time to become established before growing stems and flowers. So, the timing of your planting is everything. Once established and happy, it easily grows tall enough to produce beautiful cut flowers.

flower farmer insider tip

If farming in a cooler climate, experiment with succession planting for a longer harvest window. This flower is in demand by florists and very popular in designs for event work.

I found great value in this plant as an early season foliage even before the first bloom opens. The foliage is a nice light color with faint white speckles that is unique and adds visual interest. As I experimented with the stage of bud opening to harvest, I discovered it held up for more than 10 days, even before the buds opened.

The wavy gray-green foliage is so fluffy in a bouquet, with beautiful dangling flowers in a deep bluish purple. The stems have such a romantic presence that I love using just them in a vase. They're also lovely in garden beds and borders. It is known commonly as honeywort, a name from the European (Mediterranean) gardens where

Transplant to the garden when 3 to 5 inches tall. Pinch either 10 to 14 before or after planting in the garden. It is an excellent brancher.

ABOVE Cerinthe *'Kiwi Blue' is such a strong grower and producer that has become a leading filler for spring bouquets.*

ABOVE RIGHT *Stage to harvest: I harvest from developing buds to use as a long-lasting foliage to this bloom opening stage.*

it originated, for its sweet nectar that attracts bees, hummingbirds, and other pollinators.

- **Seeding and growing tips:** Soaking seeds in water overnight before planting can aid germination. When planting in soil blocks, push the seed deep into the block to cover the seed with soil and create darkness. Seedlings are ready to plant out when 3 to 5 inches (7.5 to 13 cm) tall, spaced 6 inches (15 cm) apart for cut flowers, 12 inches (30 cm) apart, or as desired in a garden space. Ideal growing temps are 65 to 75°F (18 to 24°C). In places with hot summers, consider planting where plants will get mid- to late-afternoon shade. I'm on the cusp of where it is reported that

Cerinthe can be fall planted, so I hoop and row cover for added protection. I also plant a second succession in very early spring, before summer warms up, to extend the harvest. I was pleasantly surprised when these young established plants faced temperatures as low as 10 to 20°F (-12 to -7°C) for days and did quite well under lightweight row covers. This plant can thrive in poor soil if it is moist but well-draining, and so should not need additional fertilization beyond standard bed prep. Pinching creates a bushier plant.

home garden tip

Consider mulching around the base of the plants to keep the soil cool and moist, which will extend the summer life of the plant. Regular cutting of old blooms can prolong flowering. Leave some seed heads in the garden to reseed for next season.

growing facts

Preferred season: Cool

Winter low temperature survival: 10°F (-12°C)

Starting from seed:
- Prefer to start seed indoors
- Start seeds 4 to 6 weeks before planting outdoors
- Prefer to start in 2-inch (5 cm) soil blocks or 128-cell plug tray
- Needs darkness to sprout; cover with ¼ inch (0.6 cm) of soil
- Soil temperature: 65°F (18C°)
- 5 to 21 days to sprout
- Air temperature for optimal transplant growth: 65 to 75°F (18 to 24°C)
- Transplant to the garden when: 3 to 5 inches (7.5 to 13 cm) tall

Sun requirement: Full sun

Height: 28 to 32 inches (70 to 80 cm)

Rows of plants per 36-inch (90 cm)-wide bed: 4

Plant spacing in row: 6 inches (15 cm)

Days to bloom: 65 to 70

Flower support: Optional

Fertilization: Standard bed preparation (see page 57)

- **Flower support notes:** Due to the nodding nature of this plant, flower support netting is beneficial to prevent toppling.

- **Harvesting and conditioning notes:** See Stage to harvest image (page 96). Harvest when the bracts darken, making the cut at ground level. Strip any bottom foliage that will be below the water level or not needed in the arrangement. I harvest in the early morning during hot conditions and take the buckets indoors to prevent wilting. *Cerinthe* may wilt in the bucket at first but can recover if allowed to rest overnight. Follow the standard conditioning steps on page 32. *Cerinthe* is not known to be ethylene sensitive. Expect fresh blooms to last 7 to 10 days in the vase.

- **Good to know:** Honeywort also works well as a subtle addition to larger mixed spring or fall flower container plantings.

Favorite Varieties

'Kiwi Blue' offers small bell-shaped purple flowers surrounded by dark blue/purple bracts, nodding above stems of wavy silvery blue-green foliage; grows about 30 inches (75 cm) tall.

97

Clarkia amoena, Clarkia unguiculata

Godetia, Satin Flower, Elegant Clarkia

We typically have this flower blooming at the very end of our spring cool-season hardy annual lineup. Native to the western United States, godetia thrives in cool to cold conditions, and even a light frost, but can't survive extended periods of freezing weather. Because of this, in most regions, it will need to be grown as a hardy annual planted in very early spring with row cover protection.

BELOW *The Godetia 'Grace Series' has multiple blooms per stem that open quickly in the heat of the day. Harvest as the first bud begins to open for fresh use. Store in a cooler to slow down opening.*

BELOW RIGHT *Transplant when 3 to 5 inches tall. It has a strong branching habit and responds well to pinching.*

- **Seeding and growing tips:** Though it may sprout in a broad range of temperatures, I've had the most success with cooler temperatures. Once sprouted, seedlings grow best with daytime temps below 75°F (24°C) and

home garden tip

The deer in our neighborhood absolutely love to munch on these plants! The row cover serves an additional purpose here. Even if you don't need it for temperature protection, if you have deer pressure, consider covering them as soon as you plant them out.

nighttime temps of 50 to 60°F (10 to 15.5°C). Because we get relatively mild winters but do experience freezing temperatures, I plant transplants in fall to get the tallest stems, and again in very early spring up to 10 weeks before my last frost date as a backup planting just in case I lose the fall planting. I use lightweight row covers to protect seedlings from cold and deer. The earlier you can plant them out before days lengthen and daytime temperatures reach 75°F (24°C), the longer the stems will be. Plant 6 inches (15 cm) apart for cut flowers. Pinching produces more stems. Additional fertilization in the field may be beneficial (nitrogen for stem growth), particularly if you start to notice browning of the lower leaves or stunted growth. Expect blooms as days lengthen past 12 hours, with multiple stems per plant, producing several flowers on each stem.

- **Flower support notes:** This plant requires support netting because the stems will be top-heavy with multiple blooms.

- **Harvesting and conditioning notes:** See Stage to harvest image (page 100). For use as fresh-cut flowers, harvest when the first flowers on a stem are open, or up to half are open.

growing facts

Preferred season: Cool

Winter low temperature survival: 20°F (-7°C)

Starting from seed:
- Prefer to start seed indoors
- Start seeds 4 to 6 weeks before planting outdoors
- Prefer to start in ¾-inch (2 cm) soil blocks
- Needs light to sprout; do not cover
- Soil temperature: 70°F (21°C)
- 10 to 14 days to sprout
- Air temperature for optimal transplant growth: 50 to 75°F (10 to 24°C)
- Transplant to the garden when: 3 to 5 inches (7.5 to 13 cm) tall

Sun requirement: Full sun, at least 6 to 8 hours

Height: 20 to 30 inches (50 to 75 cm)

Rows of plants per 36-inch (90 cm)-wide bed: 4

Plant spacing in row: 6 inches (15 cm)

Days to bloom: 75 to 85

Flower support: Yes

Fertilization: Standard bed preparation (see page 57); additional field applications may be beneficial

Elegant Salmon has long-lasting single and double blooms in a range of salmon shades that open from the bottom up. Harvest as the first few blooms begin to open. Stage to harvest on left.

Buds will continue to open and color up after cutting. For dried flower use, harvest when most of the flowers are open. Harvest the central stem at ground level and make future cuts at the base of the stem being harvested. The foliage bruises easily so most of it should be removed. Follow the standard conditioning steps on page 32. Godetia may benefit from

flower farmer insider tip

Rainstorms can severely damage flowers that are just about ready to harvest. When rain is expected, I harvest stems that are on the verge of opening a little earlier than I normally would.

holding solution, but flower food may have too much sugar in it for this plant, causing it to age prematurely. Godetia is ethylene sensitive. Remove individual blooms as they fade, and overall, you may experience a stem life (until the last bloom fades) of up to 18 days.

- **Good to know:** *Clarkia* was named after Captain William Clark, a renowned eighteenh-century leader of U.S. expeditions (of Lewis and Clark). During his travels in California and the Pacific Northwest, Captain Clark stumbled upon these plants and was so delighted that he collected their seeds to share.

Favorite Varieties

CLARKIA AMOENA
'Grace series' is a single-flowered variety that is appreciated for its taller stems. There is a nice selection of colors available, including light pink, rose pink, salmon, red, lavender, white, and a color mix. Averages fifteen stems per plant with five to six 2-inch (5 cm) blooms per stem; grows 24 to 30 inches (60 to 75 cm) tall.

CLARKIA UNGUICULATA
'Elegant Salmon' has beautiful salmon-colored blooms that begin blooming from the bottom of the stem up; grows to 36 inches (90 cm) tall.

Consolida ajacis

Larkspur

Larkspur's tall flowering spires make a great addition to spring bouquets, and the pollinators and hummingbirds love to hang out among them. I think of larkspur as "the Southerner's delphinium," because although they look similar, delphinium thrives in cooler climates and doesn't do well here. Larkspur is from the same plant family but has slightly different environmental needs. I met larkspur quite unexpectedly in my newly acquired family peony patch. The peony's transplanted roots apparently included self-sown larkspur seeds from the previous season—what a grand surprise! Larkspur and peonies make perfect companions as they bloom at about the same time.

- **Seeding and growing tips:** I store my cool-season hardy annual seeds in the freezer, but with larkspur, it is extra helpful to do this for two weeks before sowing to encourage stronger germination. We find that using fresh seed significantly improves germination rates, so we buy new seed every year. I direct seed in the garden in fall, being sure to keep the seedbed moist during sprouting. If you

home garden tip

At the end of the season, leave a few flowers to mature to reseed the garden. Any mulch in the area should be no more than 1 to 2 inches (2.5 to 5 cm) deep so fallen seeds have a chance to make contact with the soil.

Larkspur seed prefers to be planted in the garden, shown from sprouting to several weeks old.

are on the cusp of the winter low survival temperatures, it is worth experimenting with fall planting and using a floating row cover for added protection. If this flower will not survive your winter temperatures, see my special note in "Planting Seeds in the Garden" (page 48). Because larkspur needs to grow for its first six weeks at around 55°F (13°C), and for sure under 70°F (21°C) to initiate the growth of the stems and flowers, all but the coldest zones will want to plant in fall. Those with the coolest summers may be able to plant in early spring for summer blooms. Additional fertilization in the field after the soil has warmed in spring and new growth has restarted is beneficial. Once the seedlings are about 5 inches (13 cm) tall, thin them to about one every 6 inches (15 cm) for cut flowers. Side shoots don't have time to mature for us before warm weather hits, but cooler climates may have more luck with that.

growing facts

Preferred season: Cool

Winter low temperature survival: 0°F (-18°C)

Starting from seed:
- Prefer to sow directly in the field or garden
- Plant seeds 6 to 8 weeks before first fall frost
- Needs some darkness to sprout; cover only lightly
- Soil temperature: 50 to 55°F (10 to 13°C) is ideal, definitely below 65°F (18°C)
- 14 to 28 days to sprout
- Air temperature for optimal growth: 55 to 65°F (13 to 18°C)

Sun requirement: Full sun, at least 6 to 8 hours

Height: 36 to 48 inches (90 to 120 cm)

Rows of plants per 36-inch (90 cm)-wide bed: 3

Plant spacing in row: 6 inches (15 cm)

Days to bloom: 80 to 90

Flower support: Yes

Fertilization: Standard bed preparation (see page 57); additional field applications may be beneficial

- **Flower support notes:** Larkspur benefits from support netting.

- **Harvesting and conditioning notes:** See Stage to harvest image (page 103). For the best vase life, cut when the first flower on the bottom of the stem has opened. Cut the stem at ground level, and more stems will emerge from the base of the plant. Store stems upright and straight because the tips are negatively geotropic and will bend upward. This plant is highly ethylene sensitive. Follow the standard conditioning steps on page 32. Holding solution is beneficial for the top buds that will continue to color up and bloom. With proper conditioning, expect fresh blooms to last 6 to 9 days in the vase. Larkspur can also be hung to dry, in which case you'll want to harvest when most or all of the blooms are open.

- **Good to know:** All parts of the larkspur plant, including the seeds, are considered poisonous. Please use caution around pets, livestock, and children.

flower farmer insider tip

The length of stem and quality of locally grown larkspur will sweep florists off their feet! Because of high demand, I grew it in solid colors, with white, light blue, and dark blue being the bestsellers. Once I was established, my larkspur crop was sold out on standing orders each season.

Favorite Variety

'QIS™ series' produces uniform blooms and stem quality for cut flowers. The colors are available individually or as a mix, in both bright and light shades of blue, purple, pink, and white.

BELOW, FROM LEFT *Stage to harvest: Cut when the first bottom blooms open.*

From top: 'QIS™' carmine (pinks), 'QIS™' white, 'QIS™' blue, 'Misty Lavender'

Craspedia globosa

Billy Balls, Drumstick Flower

Craspedia is native to the Australian outback and, although it appreciates warmth to grow, it prefers becoming established in cool soil conditions.

home garden tip

If you don't experience freezing temperatures, you may be able to grow this as a perennial in your garden, in which case spacing farther apart (12 inches [30 cm]) is recommended. Mature plants in full bloom in the garden resemble a solar system!

It is a quirky, fun, and surprising addition to bouquets and boutonnieres. That cute little flower ball suspended above a bouquet always brings a smile, and I absolutely adore it in the garden. Billy balls is our favorite name for this on the farm, a beautiful low-growing foliage plant with silvery-green grass-like leaves and wiry tall stems that shoot up above the foliage to support a 1-inch (2.5 cm) golden ball of tiny flowers.

My first experience growing Billy was a huge success, following cool-season hardy annual recommendations. That it was easy to care for and had abundant blooms put it right at the top of my to-grow list.

Stage to harvest: Cut after the balls are yellow and start to get fuzzy. Left to right harvest stage to old.

growing facts

Preferred season: Cool

Winter low temperature survival: 10°F (-12°C)

Starting from seed:
- Prefer to start seed indoors
- Start seeds 4 to 6 weeks before planting outdoors
- Prefer to start in ¾-inch (2 cm) soil blocks
- Needs darkness to sprout; cover with soil
- Soil temperature: 70°F (21°C)
- 10 to 18 days to sprout
- Air temperature for optimal transplant growth: 70°F (21°C)
- Transplant to the garden when: 3 to 5 inches (7.5 to 13 cm) tall or wide

Sun requirement: Full sun

Height: 24 to 26 inches (30 to 35 cm)

Rows of plants per 36-inch (90 cm)-wide bed: 4

Plant spacing in row: 6 inches (15 cm)

Days to bloom: 110 to 120

Flower support: Optional

Fertilization: Standard bed preparation (see page 57); additional field applications may be beneficial

- **Seeding and growing tips:** Sow seeds into ¾-inch (2 cm) soil blocks, pushing the seed down into the block to cover it lightly with soil. They are ready to plant when the leaves are 3 to 5 inches (7.5 to 13 cm) tall with the foliage growing more out than up at first. *Craspedia* likes well-drained soil, so a raised bed is ideal. Stems emerge from the plant base and produce a single globe covered in tiny flowers, so pinching is not required. Expect several stems per plant. We're at the edge of the regions where this plant can grow as a perennial, which is what led me to experiment with growing it as a hardy annual. We find that fall-planted seedlings produce the tallest stems, so I plant in fall and use lightweight row cover to give added protection. Winter row cover protection also helps deter deer—they tend to really like this plant's foliage. I have good results from succession planting this flower, following the fall planting with a very early spring planting.

- **Flower support notes:** Netting is optional as the stiff nature of these strong stems and the small blooms tend to keep them upright.

- **Harvesting and conditioning notes:** See Stage to harvest image (page 104). Harvest when the majority or all of the tiny blooms are open and the ball is uniformly golden in color. Make the cut at or near ground level; additional stems will emerge from the base of the plant. There is little to no stripping required, except at the very end of the stem, so this is a quick and easy flower to harvest. Follow the standard conditioning steps on page 32. *Craspedia* does not require any special holding treatment and is not known to be ethylene sensitive. Expect fresh blooms to last 7 to 14 days in the vase, or hang blooms upside-down to dry and enjoy them indefinitely.

flower farmer insider tip

Florists love these! They give any arrangement a modern pop of color. They also hold up well out of water for events and can be dried easily when hung upside-down. Although these blooms may be on the small side of the cut flowers we grow, their round shape adds so much texture and interest, whether fresh or dried.

- **Good to know:** Deer seem very attracted to these on our property so we spread row cover over them as soon as they're planted in fall.

Favorite Varieties

'Golden Drumstick' is a good cut flower used fresh or dried; grows 24 to 36 inches (60 to 90 cm) tall.

'Sun Ball' is a variety quite popular with cut-flower growers and is another one that is excellent used as a fresh or dried flower; grows 20 to 30 inches (50 75 cm) tall.

BELOW, FROM LEFT *Transplant when 3 to 5 inches tall and protect from deer who love this foliage.*

A beautiful, long-stemmed bunch of 'Sunny Ball' grown by Young's Mill Flower Farm, Newport News, VA.

Cynoglossum amabile

Chinese Forget-Me-Not, Blue Showers, Hound's Tongue

You may be familiar with traditional forget-me-nots, a biennial flower often spotted along the borders of wooded areas. Chinese forget-me-nots are a different, but similar-looking, plant that produces lovely true blue sprays of flowers (*"amabile"* means "lovely") but grows as a cool-season hardy annual instead of a biennial, so it blooms in its first year of growth. There's a pink version, too, so you can choose either or

both to coordinate with the rest of your garden plantings or bouquet elements. We love this as a spring filler flower, and the bees love this one, too, so it's great for the pollinator garden as well!

- **Seeding and growing tips:** Chinese forget-me-nots don't tolerate hot summers, so where I live, my main opportunity to grow them is as a fall-planted cool-season hardy annual. I direct seed in fall, seeding heavily in three rows per bed so I can weed around them with a standup hoe. If you're on the cusp of their lowest winter survival temperatures, I encourage you to try planting them in fall

home garden tip

Chinese forget-me-nots are also good for containers!

Seeds planted in the garden from just sprouted to several weeks old.

growing facts

Preferred season: Cool

Winter low temperature survival: 0°F (-18°C)

Starting from seed:
- Prefer to sow directly in the field or garden
- Plant seeds 6 to 8 weeks before first fall frost
- Needs light to sprout; do not cover
- Soil temperature: 70°F (21°C)
- 2 to 3 days to sprout
- Air temperature for optimal growth: 70°F (21°C)

Sun requirement: Full sun/part shade

Height: 18 to 24 inches (45 to 60 cm)

Rows of plants per 36-inch (90 cm)-wide bed: 3

Plant spacing in row: 6 inches (15 cm)

Days to bloom: 80 to 90

Flower support: Optional

Fertilization: Standard bed preparation (see page 57); additional field applications may be beneficial

with hoop and row cover protection to get them through. If this flower will not survive your winter temperatures, see my special note in "Planting Seeds in the Garden" (page 48). Fall-planted seedlings may benefit from additional fertilization in the field after the soil has warmed in spring and new growth has restarted. In spring, once the seedlings are about 5 inches (13 cm) tall, thin them with a hoe to about one every 6 inches (15 cm). We do not pinch these since these are already

short plants. Instead, the first center stem cut serves as the pinch, and side shoots may develop (depending on how quickly our summers warm up). Growers in warmer climates may experience shorter stems and may have more success when planted in a spot with mid- to late-afternoon shade.

- **Flower support notes:** The plant's shorter nature means you may not need support netting.

- **Harvesting and conditioning notes:** See Stage to harvest image (page 109). Depending on your use, harvest when one-third to one-half of the florets on the stem have opened. Flowers continue to open after cutting. Harvest the central stem almost at ground level, just above the lowest three or four side shoots. Future harvests can be made at the base of the stem. To help avoid wilting, I strip all the foliage below the bloom, harvest during the coolest part of the day, and allow cuts to rest in water for at least a few hours before arranging. Follow the standard conditioning steps on page 32. This plant seems to benefit from the use of holding solution. It is not known to be ethylene sensitive. Expect fresh blooms to last 5 to 7 days in the vase with proper conditioning.

- **Good to know:** The wild biennial version of this plant may be considered invasive in areas where it thrives. However, the varieties recommended were developed specifically for use as cut flowers. Though they may reseed in ideal conditions, they are not enthusiastic spreaders like their wilder cousins.

flower farmer insider tip

This plant is one of very few with true blue flowers, which is a color always in high demand. So even though it can be on the shorter side for a cut flower, its blue color makes it worthy to grow in my book. In cooler climates, experiment with planting both in fall and spring for two successions.

'**Firmament**' is the best blue variety for cut-flower use, with tall stems and good branching after the center stem is cut; grows 24 to 36 inches (60 to 90 cm) tall.

'**Mystery Rose**' produces dainty pale-pink flowers on sturdy stems; grows 24 to 30 inches (60 to 75 cm) tall.

Favorite Varieties

'**Blue Chinese Forget-Me-Nots**' is a soft blue bloom on potentially shorter stems; grows 18 to 24 inches (45 to 60 cm) tall.

BELOW, FROM LEFT *Stage to harvest: Cut when the first few flowers are opening.*

An early vase of 'Firmament' and 'Mystery Rose.' I have found that stems grow taller as the season progresses.

Dianthus, Dianthus barbatus, Dianthus caryophyllus

Sweet William, Carnation

Dianthus is a large family of plants full of beautiful, sturdy flowers. Some make excellent cut flowers, others have pretty flowers but their stems are too short, and then there are those that require more than one season to bloom because they are biennials, not annuals. Perhaps a bit confusing at first, but it's worth finding those that are a good fit for your garden. There are also perennial types of *Dianthus* sold as bedding plants—those will be much shorter plants. To ensure that you reap a bounty of cut flowers, select varieties carefully. Those that I grow are specifically hybridized for use as cut flowers.

The strong growing and winter survival habits of this family fueled my fire to pursue cool-season hardy annuals. I have grown many different *Dianthus* in our cutting gardens, and there are a few that have proven to be reliable producers, easy to grow, and excellent cuts. This hardy plant attracts bees, birds, and butterflies. Some plants' blooms are fragrant, smelling spicy like cloves.

I grow three different types of *Dianthus*: Sweet William, both the true annual varieties (quicker to bloom) and a biennial variety (takes longer to bloom), plus I grow heirloom carnations. Each plant group fills a unique spot in my spring and summer harvests. Because of the vast variety of colors, the

home garden tip

Consider growing the biennial 'Electron' among your permanent perennial plantings and allow it to reseed after the initial planting. To encourage reseeding, leave some of the blooms on the plants to develop and scatter seed. The seeds will need to make contact with soil, so mulch should be fairly light. Scout for seedlings in late summer and fall.

BELOW, FROM LEFT *Tranpslant when 3 to 5 inches tall.*

Stage to harvest: Make the cut from no blooms to use as filler, up to a third of the blooms open.

sturdiness of the stems, long vase life, and the sweet fragrance, dianthus is a popular cut flower.

Annual Sweet William: A true annual that does not require a cold period to bloom and can be succession planted. For top-quality tall stems, include a fall planting where it can survive your lowest winter temperatures. This type is a great candidate for succession planting in fall, winter, very early spring, spring, and summer. Skip fall and winter planting where winter temperatures dip below the survival lows. Once you find the earliest and latest times to plant in your conditions, these annuals can provide a wide window of harvest of this in-demand cash crop.

Biennial Sweet William: Requires a cold period after the transplants are established in the garden to produce flowers the following spring; this is called "vernalization." Plant transplants in late summer and early fall to receive the required 40°F (4°C) or colder temperatures for several weeks to produce flowers the following spring. Biennials do not follow a succession plan.

Carnations: This annual does not require a cold period to bloom. It can be a short-lived perennial in areas with cool summer months with moist conditions and excellent drainage.

- **Seeding and growing tips:** Sow seeds firmly on the surface of the soil blocks. Place on a wire cooling rack set on top of the heat mat (see Cool-Season Tips, page 64). Seeds sown on the soil's surface need to be kept moist, so I lay wide-weave burlap over the blocks until the seeds start to crack. The Sweet William types can be pinched to encourage branching and may result in an additional four to six blooms per plant. Carnations have a strong branching habit without pinching (see "Pinching Plants," page 53). Because they are relatively long-lived, these plants benefit from additional fertilization in the spring

growing facts

Preferred season: Cool

Winter low temperature survival: -10°F (-23°C)

Starting from seed:
- Prefer to start seed indoors
- Start seed indoors 4 to 6 weeks before planting outdoors
- Prefer to start in ¾-inch (2 cm) soil blocks
- Needs light to sprout; do not cover
- Soil temperature: 65 to 70°F (18 to 21°C)
- 7 to 14 days to sprout
- Air temperature for optimal transplant growth: 55 to 60°F (13 to 15.5°C)
- Transplant to the garden when: 3 to 5 inches (7.5 to 13 cm) tall

Sun requirement: Minimum 8 hours, more is better

Height: 18 to 36 inches (45 to 90 cm), depending on variety and conditions

Rows of plants per 36-inch (90 cm)-wide bed: 4

Plant spacing in row: 6 inches (15 cm)

Days to bloom: 105 to 140, depending on variety and conditions

Flower support: Yes

Fertilization: Standard bed preparation (see page 57); additional field applications are beneficial

after the weather has warmed and plants begin to show growth again. Rust can develop but typically affects only the lower leaves. Rust has never been an issue for us since we strip the lower leaves off at harvest.

- **Flower support notes:** I use flower support netting on all *Dianthus* plantings. The varieties that we grow have strong stems but the flower heads are heavy and go down easily in rain and wind.

- **Harvesting and conditioning notes:** See Stage to harvest image (page 110). Depending on your use, you may cut when one-third of the flowers in a cluster have opened. Make the first cut of the central stem almost at ground level, just above the lowest two or three side shoots. Any future cuts should be made at the stem's base. I remove the leaves from the bottom few inches of the stem and find it hydrates easily. Sweet William is ethylene sensitive, meaning that the ethylene produced by other cut flowers, fruits, and vegetables in storage will shorten its vase life. The flowers benefit from the use of holding solution. Blooms are long lasting in the vase, typically 7 to 12 days.

- **Good to know:** I grow the Sweet William type for more than its flowers: I harvest it before it shows any buds to use as green filler in mixed spring bouquets. The petals of Sweet William are edible once removed from the base (which can be bitter) and are commonly used to top cold drinks, desserts, and salads.

flower farmer insider tip

Sweet William is a crop in much demand for commercial customers. Florists use it daily and, because of its long vase life, it is excellent for making bouquets for supermarkets. The quality of locally grown stems is so superior to those shipped in that it is a great crop to produce as early and late in the season as possible.

Favorite Varieties

DIANTHUS X BARBATUS:
No Cold Period Required

'Amazon series' is an annual that does not require a cold period. It features tall, sturdy plants with more branching and clusters of blooms that are less densely packed than other varieties. This series is excellent for succession planting from fall, where it survives winter low temperatures, through summer, and tends to be more heat tolerant than others. It produces good stem length even on later plantings and comes in solid colors of purple, cherry, and 'Neon Rose Magic'; grows 18 to 30 inches (45 to 75 cm) tall.

'Dynasty series' is an annual that does not require a cold period. It has many double ruffled blooms on well-branched heads. It is available in orchid, purple, red, rose lace, and white blush; grows 20 inches (50 cm) tall.

DIANTHUS BARBATUS
No Cold Period Required

'Sweet series' is an annual that does not require a cold period. Its blooms have densely packed,

rounded clusters on slightly shorter stems. This series can be succession planted; however, in my outdoor growing conditions, I plant in fall to get the tallest stems. It blooms in solid colors including white, red, coral, scarlet, black cherry, pink, and some bicolor combinations; grows 18 to 24 inches (45 to 60 cm) tall.

'Bodestolz mix' is an annual that does not require a cold period. It is a mix of stunning bicolor ball-shaped blooms on strong, upright stems. It can be succession planted, with my best stem lengths resulting from fall plantings; grows roughly 28 inches (70 cm) tall.

Cold Period Required

'Electron mix' is a biennial that does require a cold period. The strong growth habit and winter hardiness of this variety make it an all-time favorite of flower farmers. The beautiful 3-inch (7.5 cm) vivid bicolor blooms in umbrella-shaped clusters sit atop sturdy stems. 'Electron' can be a strong reseeder where it is happy. This habit may be convenient in the home cutting garden, but the farmer should replant each year to ensure a good stand of plants for this significant crop; grows 20 to 30 inches (50 to 75 cm) tall.

ABOVE, FROM LEFT Sweet William 'Amazon' develops buds and blooms later so I often use it at this stage and a little later as a long-lasting filler

Sweet William 'Sweet' includes many colors, has a ball type bloom, and is the first to bloom in my garden.

Sweet William 'Electron' is widely grown by farmers for its dynamite colors. This variety must be transplanted in late summer to receive the required cold period to bloom the following spring as does 'Super Duplex.'

Carnation, 'Chabaud' includes a wide range of solid and bicolor blooms. It has a sweet and spicy fragrance that is a nice touch in spring bouquets.

DIANTHUS CARYOPHYLLUS
No Cold Period Required

'Chabaud' is an annual that does not require a cold period. Although these sweet, frilly blooms are not as large and showy as the common carnations used by florists, 'Chabaud' brings to a spring bouquet what they don't—a sweet clove fragrance. This French heirloom is also a great ingredient for boutonnieres. The series includes 'Marie' (pale yellow), 'La France' (blush pink), 'Striped & Picotee mix', 'Benigna' (white with red stripes), 'Orange Sherbet', and 'Jeanne Dionis' (white); grows 20 to 30 inches (50 to 75 cm) tall.

Digitalis purpurea

Foxglove

Foxglove is such a lovely and whimsical flower! I love all the little details of freckling on these tubular blossoms. The hummingbirds and bees particularly love *Digitalis*. And the deer don't really bother it, at least not that I've seen in my garden.

There are two different types of *Digitalis*: perennial and biennial. Most of the older varieties you may be familiar with as cottage garden plants are biennials; they grow vegetation in their first year of life and then flower in their second year, go to seed, and reseed the garden for next year. So, gardeners can maintain a nice patch of biennial foxglove for many years, if conditions are good for reseeding.

The second type of foxglove is what I grow. It is considered a "tender perennial." In other words, not a long-lived perennial so I grow it as a cool-season hardy annual. This type flowers in its first year of growth, making great cut flowers. All the varieties that I recommend are the type that flower in their first year of growth.

Transplant when leaves reach 3 to 5 inches long.

They can be fall planted and produce blooms the following spring or planted in very early spring to bloom in early summer. Sadly, that spring blooming plant rarely survives my brutal summers, so we count on replanting each fall.

- **Seeding and growing tips:** Sow seeds on the surface of ¾-inch (2 cm) soil blocks; do not cover. Keep the soil and seeds moist before germination; we cover trays with wide-weave burlap to help with this. They're ready to plant when the leaves are 3 to 5 inches (7.5 to 13 cm) tall. Plant in a spot that will receive 4 to 8 hours of sunlight with mid- to late-afternoon shade. Space plants 6 inches (15 cm) apart for cut flowers, 12 inches (30 cm) in the landscape. Fall-planted seedlings can benefit from the application of a balanced liquid fertilizer in spring once soil has warmed and growth has restarted. Stems emerge from the plant base, so pinching is not required. Expect two to four stems per plant.

- **Flower support notes:** The flower stalks are strong, but when full of buds they're likely to topple over in the field during wind or storms unless they have adequate flower support netting.

- **Harvesting and conditioning notes:** See Stage to harvest image (page 116). Harvest when the first flower on the stem opens; the other flowers will continue to open. Make the cut at ground level. Store them upright in a bucket to avoid curving of the stems. Follow the standard conditioning steps on page 32. Like other spike-form flowers, foxglove is ethylene sensitive. Cut stems benefit from the use of holding solution, typically improving vase life by a couple of days. Expect fresh blooms to last 7 to 9 days in the vase.

growing facts

Preferred season: Cool

Winter low temperature survival: -10°F (-23°C)

Starting from seed:
- Prefer to start seed indoors
- Start seeds 4 to 6 weeks before planting outdoors
- Prefer to start in ¾-inch (2 cm) soil blocks
- Needs light to sprout; do not cover
- Soil temperature: 65 to 70°F (18 to 21°C)
- 7 to 14 days to sprout
- Air temperature for optimal transplant growth: 60 to 65°F (15.5 to 18°C)
- Transplant to the garden when: 3 to 5 inches (7.5 to 13 cm) tall/wide

Sun requirement: Part sun, 4 to 8 hours

Height: 24 to 48 inches (60 to 120 cm)

Rows of plants per 36-inch (90 cm)-wide bed: 4

Plant spacing in row: 6 inches (15 cm)

Days to bloom: 120 to 135

Flower support: Yes

Fertilization: Standard bed preparation (see page 57); additional field applications may be beneficial

flower farmer insider tip

Foxglove is the flower I can thank for getting my foot in the door at Colonial Williamsburg. 'Foxy' swept them off their feet, and they became one of my largest customers for more than a decade.

RIGHT, FROM TOP *Stage to harvest: 'Foxy' harvested when the bottom first few flowers are opening.*

RIGHT, FROM TOP *Stage to harvest: 'Foxy' harvested when the bottom first few flowers are opening.*

Gorgeous Digitalis 'Dalmatian' peach and cream grown by Wind Haven Farm, King William, VA

- **Good to know:** All parts of the plant are considered poisonous; please use caution around pets, livestock, and children.

Favorite Varieties

'Camelot' features softer colors including lavender, cream, rose, and white. This variety produces good side shoots that give the plant a fuller look in the garden; grows 28 to 40 inches (70 to 100 cm) tall.

'Dalmatian' produces flowers bunched more closely together and gives a fuller look in a bouquet; grows 24 to 36 inches (60 to 90 cm) tall.

'Foxy' produces 2- to 3-inch (5 to 7.5 cm)-long funnel-shaped blooms in mauve, white, creamy yellow, and pink—all with maroon spots; grows 24 to 36 inches (60 to 90 cm) tall.

home garden tip

Foxglove is a very prolific bloomer if conditions are right (mid- to late-afternoon shade) and if faded blooms are removed promptly. In the landscape, foxglove looks great against a dark background such as a wall or shrub; it can also be grown in containers.

Eustoma grandiflorum

Lisianthus

"Is that a rose? It's lovely!" In my experience lisianthus is often mistaken for a rose, and with good reason. Although it originates from the wildflower known as Texas bluebells, today's hybrid varieties have high petal counts and come in a broad range of colors. Many very closely resemble roses (particularly spray roses) but without those pesky thorns! Flower farmers affectionately call lisianthus "Lizzie," as if she is an old friend.

Lisianthus is often grown in hoops or greenhouses, but growing it outdoors in a garden is definitely doable. It can be worthwhile for the home gardener and profitable for the flower farmer.

This is one of the few cool-season hardy annuals that likes a cool start yet has a hot finish, meaning it prefers to be planted into cool to cold soil, yet blooms and thrives during the heat of summer. I consider Lizzie a key flower for the mid- to late-summer bouquet, and it is in high demand from commercial customers. There is such a big difference between locally grown Lizzie and what is shipped in from distant lands. The homegrown stems can be left on the plant for more blooms to open before harvesting, whereas those from far away must be cut in bud stage to prevent damage during shipping. More open blooms at harvest make for a jaw-dropping cut flower and add great value per stem when used in bouquets or bunching for commercial customers.

For many of us, successfully growing Lizzie in the garden requires starting with purchased plants. Why? Because these transplants require very specific and somewhat difficult growing conditions, and when they don't get it, they tend to hold a grudge. They express their

Transplant when 2 to 3 inches tall.

ABOVE, FROM LEFT *Stage to harvest: I prefer to harvest when 3 to 4 blooms are open (on left), but if rain is coming, cut them when 1 to 2 are open (on right). 'Rosanne' green.*

Left to right: 'Voyage' champagne, 'Mariachi' white, 'Rosanne' green, and 'Voyage' deep rose

Lisianthus blooms may appear delicate, but they bloom in the heat of the summer and often last beyond two weeks in the vase. 'Voyage' champagne and 'Mariachi' white.

home garden tip

In addition to the online sources listed in the Resources section (page 230), reach out to your locally owned nursery to see if they sell lisianthus seedlings in spring. Some nurseries purchase tiny plugs in winter and grow them into the spring, then sell them as larger seedlings.

dissatisfaction by not growing up and blooming as expected—a heartbreaker for the gardener who spent months growing them. I consider growing Lizzie from seed to be more "graduate level" work; see the seeding and growing tips following before tackling it. I find growing Lizzie simple and successful, if I've started with well-grown, healthy transplants.

- **Seeding and growing tips:** Getting lisianthus seed to germinate isn't the big challenge; it is the 8 to 12 weeks of growing the transplant to a plantable size that is. This long growing period provides plenty of opportunities to accidentally kill those babies or to fail to meet their temperature and watering requirements, causing long-term negative effects. Lisianthus seedlings need to be kept relatively cool, under 75°F (24°C) for sure, before being transplanted or they can suffer from "rosetting," which is a type of stunting resulting in low vegetative growth instead of long stems with flowers. I have firsthand experience with rosetting, and it is incredibly

growing facts

Preferred season: Cool

Winter low temperature survival: 0°F (-18°C)

Starting from seed:
- Prefer to start seed indoors
- Start seed indoors 12 to 16 weeks before planting outdoors
- Prefer to start in ¾-inch (2 cm) soil blocks
- Needs light to sprout; do not cover
- Soil temperature: 70°F (21°C)
- 7 to 14 days to sprout
- Air temperature for optimal transplant growth: 60 to 75°F (15.5 to 24°C)
- Transplant to the garden when: 2 to 3 inches (5 to 7.5 cm) tall

Sun requirement: Full sun

Height: 24 to 42 inches (60 to 105 cm)

Rows of plants per 36-inch (90 cm)-wide bed: 9

Plant spacing in row: 6 inches (15 cm)

Days to bloom: 150 to 170 days

Flower support: Yes

Fertilization: Standard bed preparation (see page 57); additional field applications may be beneficial

disappointing after months of effort. That is why flower farmers who depend on a strong crop harvest should consider purchasing transplants when growing this flower (see Resources, page 230, for home gardeners and flower farmers plant sources).

Lisianthus can be susceptible to several root diseases, so excellent drainage is a must. This flower survives my winter low temperatures, making fall planting an option. However, I opt to plant in very early spring to avoid the risk of constant wet soil conditions during winter growing. Pinching does encourage additional branching but is not mandatory because lisianthus branches naturally. Perhaps my most abundant harvest of lisianthus stems came the year we had a hard freeze 2 weeks after our last historical frost date, killing thousands of the central stems on my transplants back to ground level. Although I was initially devastated, the plants were not dead and regrew a bumper crop, producing three or four major stems per plant. Sometimes, what seems a potential big loss turns into the lesson of a lifetime. I give a hard pinch to 50 percent of my plants, just above the bottom two leaves, when they are 6 to 8 inches (15 to 20 cm) tall. Don't be afraid to plant these flowers close together. Lisianthus plants do not grow a dense canopy of foliage, so closer spacing works to encourage taller stems and helps to out-compete weed growth.

119

flower farmer insider tip

Buying plugs saves time and space in your grow room, as well as gives you reliable transplants that will perform and produce. Make sure you order early, though! Plug growers only start what is presold, meaning they plant for you when you order. So you'll need to order lisianthus at least 12 to 16 weeks (how long it takes to grow) before the date you want your seedlings to ship. Find plant sources in the Resources section (page 230).

- **Flower support notes:** Flower support netting is recommended with support posts 4 feet apart to be sure you have a strong framework for the heavy canopy of blooms. Although some varieties are taller than others, they all produce multiple blooms on single stems, about half of which will be open before cutting. That creates a heavy canopy. The stems are sturdy but brittle, so in wind and storms they may snap off or be flattened and then grow crooked.

- **Harvesting and conditioning notes:** See Stage to harvest image (page 118). Resist the urge to harvest the entire stem when that first bloom opens. Either disbud or leave it blooming on the stem, or if the single stem under that bloom is long enough, you can snip a handful and make what we call the "Lizzie bouquet," perfect for a small, short vase and commanding a price comparable to our full-size mixed bouquets. The subsequent blooms will come on much taller stems and are typically ready to harvest 5 to 7 days after you see that first bloom. Wait until roughly

half of the blooms on the stem have opened. Be aware that rain causes water spots on dark-colored petals, so watch the weather closely and harvest before open blooms risk being damaged. Harvest just above the bottom two to four leaves on the plant to encourage additional flushes of blooms with good stem length. Depending on the length of your season, you may get a second or even third flush of flowers if you keep them harvested and weed-free.

Lisianthus benefits from traditional conditioning steps, including holding solution and flower food in the vase, which allows buds at the top of the stem to continue to color up and open. It is also ethylene sensitive. Lisianthus is a tough flower with an amazing vase life, typically 7 to 14 days. They also hold up very well out of water, especially in bud stage, so they're great for use in boutonnieres, corsages, and such.

- **Good to know:** Lisianthus varieties have a designated group number, which indicates how soon it is expected to flower. This is a good indicator for stem length. Group 1 is an early bloomer, which can mean shorter stems; Group 4 is a later bloomer, increasing the likelihood of longer stems. I have found that Groups 3 and 4 give more time for my very early spring plantings to grow taller before they bloom. Some varieties are offered in several groups.

Favorite Varieties

'**ABC series**' is the most reliable variety we grow, both in terms of stem length and hardiness. It features double blooms with high petal counts. It tends to bloom 1 to 2 weeks earlier than other similar varieties and was bred for a reduced likelihood of rosetting. The series has lots of colors, including white, yellow, green, and multiple shades of pink and purple; grows 36 to 45 inches (90 to 113 cm) tall.

'Echo' was developed for the cut-flower market; this one feature large double blooms with strong flower stalks in colors of white, yellow, peach, champagne, and purple. It falls on the shorter side though, at 24 to 34 inches (60 to 85 cm) tall.

'Mariachi' produces 2- to 3-inch (5 to 7.5 cm) extra double (very high petal count, many rows of petals) blooms in colors of white, yellow, green, bicolor, and shades of pink and purple; grows 30 to 38 inches (75 to 95 cm) tall.

'Rosanne' has become popular mostly for its unique colors, currently the only one to offer the antique-looking muted mauve/tan color called "brown." These are very popular for wedding work. It blooms fuller and denser than some other varieties; grows 30 to 36 inches (75 to 90 cm) tall.

BELOW, FROM LEFT *A bed of newly planted Lisianthus transplants in February planted into biodegradable mulch film with the black side up to help warm the soil. Eight rows across the 30-inch-wide bed with plants 6 inches apart in the row.*

Blooms become heavy and susceptible to falling over in rain and wind as they near harvest stage so I use flower-support netting. Half of this bed was pinched 10 days after planting. The pinched ones are in the front, and those not pinched are in the back.

Gypsophila elegans

Annual Baby's Breath, Showy Baby's Breath, "Gyp," Maiden's Breath

You're probably familiar with perennial baby's breath—those tiny white tufts that are so commonly seen dried and used in wedding work and corsages. It's been a mainstay of the floral industry for decades. Perennial baby's breath thrives in cooler climates, but it's not a plant that will survive my brutally hot summers. Instead, I grow baby's breath as a fall-planted cool-season hardy annual, and it's a great addition to our lineup. Annual baby's breath has a different look to it because the flowers are single blooms and open-face, with a growth habit that is looser, creating a more casual feel.

- **Seeding and growing tips:** Baby's breath seeds are tiny and should be covered only very lightly with soil. I do this by pushing the seed deeper into the soil block, which

creates darkness. Keep the soil and seeds moist before germination; we cover trays with wide-weave burlap to help with this. The growing seedlings are particularly susceptible to damping off, so be sure soil blocks dry out completely between waterings. They're ready to plant out when 3 to 5 inches (7.5 to 13 cm) tall, spaced 6 inches (15 cm) apart for cut flowers or further apart as desired in a garden space. In places with hot summers, consider planting where it will get mid- to late-afternoon shade. This plant is a fast grower and tolerates poor soil as long as it drains well, so it shouldn't need fertilizer beyond standard bed preparation. In fact, too much fertility may result in taller, spindly plants that topple over easily. Stems emerge from the plant base, so pinching is not required. Expect multiple stems per plant.

- **Flower support notes:** I use flower support netting on my fall plantings because their stems are so much taller, often reaching 30 inches (75 cm) tall. Without support, they can easily go down in rain or wind.

- **Harvesting and conditioning notes:** See Stage to harvest image (far left on this page. Harvest when the first flowers on the stem crack open, making the cut at ground level. Strip everything 6 inches (15 cm) or so below the top of the stem. I harvest in the early morning during hot conditions and take the buckets indoors to prevent wilting. Follow

FROM FAR LEFT *Stage to harvest: Cut when a third of the tiny flowers on the stem are open.*

Transplant when 5 inches tall. These plants tend to branch naturally and don't need pinching.

growing facts

Preferred season: Cool

Winter low temperature survival: 10°F (-12°C)

Starting from seed:
- Prefer to start seed indoors
- Start seeds 4 to 6 weeks before planting outdoors
- Prefer to start in ¾-inch (2 cm) soil blocks
- Needs darkness to sprout; cover very lightly with soil
- Soil temperature: 70°F (21°C)
- 7 to 14 days to sprout
- Air temperature for optimal transplant growth: 60 to 65°F (15.5 to 18°C)
- Transplant to the garden when: 3 to 5 inches (7.5 to 13 cm) tall

Sun requirement: Full sun

Height: 18 to 30 inches (45 to 75 cm)

Rows of plants per 36-inch (90 cm)-wide bed: 4

Plant spacing in row: 6 inches (15 cm)

Days to bloom: 45 to 60

Flower support: Yes

Fertilization: Standard bed preparation (see page 67)

home garden tip

The billowy growth habit of baby's breath can soften the edges of a container, garden space, or rock feature. Leave a few blooms on the plants to encourage reseeding.

the standard conditioning steps on page 32. Cut stems benefit from the use of holding solution and flower food so flowers continue to open. *Gypsophila* is ethylene sensitive. Expect fresh blooms to last 10 to 14 days in the vase.

- **Good to know:** The name "*Gypsophila*" means "gypsum loving," a description of the soil conditions they thrive in.

Favorite Varieties

'Covent Garden' offers dainty white open-face flowers on airy branched stems, great for use as a bouquet filler; grows up to 36 inches (90 cm) tall.

Annual Baby's Breath has so many tiny open blooms that they make excellent stand-alone bouquets and a great spring filler.

flower farmer insider tip

Even with my early warm summers, I have had success with succession planting annual *Gypsophila*. I plant my transplants in the fall 6 to 8 weeks before the first expected fall frost. This planting produces the earliest and most abundant stems, often reaching a height of 30 inches (75 cm). Because it is a white flower blooming in spring during the highest demand, I always try for a second planting in my efforts to extend the harvest season. I try to have transplants closer to the 5-inch (13 cm)-tall size ready to plant in very early spring, which is 6 to 8 weeks before my last frost. They may not produce stems as tall or robust as the fall planting does, but the stems are very usable. If farming in a cooler climate, experiment with succession planting every couple of weeks for a longer harvest window.

Lathyrus odoratus

Sweet Pea

Sweet peas have an intoxicating fragrance, gorgeous delicate tendrils, and a beautiful, romantic flower form. As a beginner flower farmer, I stumbled onto learning how to grow them in my southern climate and have successfully made them part of my gardens ever since.

In recent years, I have tweaked my growing methods thanks to the guidance of my flower-farming friend and horticulturist Bailey Hale. Based on his research, I no longer soak seeds before planting, and I follow his temperature guidance for sprouting and growing sweet pea transplants. Sweet pea lovers everywhere are thrilled that Bailey is devoting the majority of his efforts to the production and preservation of top-quality sweet pea seed.

There are several types of sweet peas, some with larger blooms, others with more fragrance. They have varied blooming times. When selecting which to grow, gardeners in southern climates may want to lean to spring-flowering plants because, sadly, the summer-flowering types are not heat tolerant.

- **Flower support notes:** Sweet peas require sturdy vertical support netting or a trellis to wrap their tendrils around.

- **Harvesting and conditioning notes:** See Stage to harvest image (page 126). Harvest when all blooms are open except the top two flowers; flowers do not continue to open after cutting. Make the cut at the base of the stem, where it connects to the vine. Follow the standard conditioning steps on page 32. Although they benefit from holding solution

Transplant vines when they reach 3 to 5 inches.

flower farmer insider tip with
Bailey Hale, Ardelia Farm & Co.

"Sweet peas are not difficult to grow from seed; they are simply specific in what they like. Understanding their needs allows you to give them what they want. Sweet peas like it cold, so keep these temperature ranges in mind . . ."

- 50 to 55°F (10 to 13°C) for germination
- 35 to 50°F (2 to 10°C) for bulking up (cold snaps down to 20°F [-7°C] are fine!)
- 45 to 70°F (7 to 21°C) for optimal flowering
- 65°F (18°C) days with 45°F (7°C) nights are ideal

Sweet peas seed sourcing can be found in the Resources section (page 230).

growing facts

Preferred season: Cool

Winter low temperature survival:
10°F (-12°C)

Starting from seed:
- Prefer to start seed indoors
- Start seed indoors 3 weeks before planting outdoors
- Prefer to start in 2-inch (5 cm) soil blocks
- Needs darkness to sprout; cover with soil, about ½ inch (1 cm) deep
- Soil temperature: 50 to 55°F (10 to 13°C)
- 7 to 10 days to sprout
- Air temperature for optimal transplant growth: 35 to 50°F (2 to 10°C)
- Transplant to the garden when: 3 to 5 inches (7.5 to 13 cm) tall

Sun requirement: Full sun, at least 8 hours per day

Height: Vines 36 to 72 inches (90 to 180 cm), stems 8 to 14 inches (20 to 35 cm)

Rows of plants per 36-inch (90 cm)-wide bed: 2 (on either side of a trellis)

Plant spacing in row: 12 inches (30 cm)

Days to bloom: 75 to 90 days

Flower support: Vertical support required

Fertilization: Standard bed preparation (see page 57); additional field applications may be beneficial

home garden tip

If you don't intend to cut them regularly for bouquets, remove the old blooms to keep new flowers coming.

and flower food, flowers should be sold or enjoyed as soon as possible after cutting for maximum fragrance and vase life. Expect fresh blooms to last 5 to 7 days in the vase.

- **Good to know:** Sweet peas are not edible, and some parts of the plant are considered toxic. They are deer resistant.

Favorite Varieties

'Alison Louise' is summer-flowering with light to medium blue blooms.

'Betty White' is summer-flowering with white bloom with navy stripes.

flower farmer insider tip

If flower stems are short, I harvest vines with several blooming flowers to use in bouquets. Vines can also be used without blooms as foliage.

'**Enigma**' is summer flowering with marbled pink blooms and a strong fragrance.

'**High Scent**' is spring-flowering with highly fragrant 1- to 2-inch (2.5 to 5 cm) white flowers with lavender tips.

'**Kiera Madeline**' is summer-flowering with cream blooms with pink picotee.

'**Mammoth Mix**' blooms in spring in colors of rose, salmon, scarlet, white, and lavender.

'**Royal Mix**' is spring-flowering with fragrant 1- to 2-inch (2.5 to 5 cm) flowers in purple, red, pink, and white.

'**Spring Sunshine Cerise**' is summer-flowering with magenta blooms.

'**Spring Sunshine Peach**' is summer-flowering with light salmon blooms.

BELOW, FROM LEFT *Stage to harvest: Two ways to harvest sweet peas: either harvest the vine with several flower stems that have developed flowers or harvest the shorter individual flower stems.*

'Spring Sunshine Peach' sweet pea blooms and seed grown by Bailey Haley of Ardelia Farm & Co.

Limonium sinuatum

Statice

In my earlier growing years, I didn't have much luck with statice—it would always bloom on very short stems. But when I read a grower's comment about successfully wintering over a good portion of his statice crop, I thought, "It's a hardy annual??" No wonder I hadn't been able to grow it all these years! I had been planting and treating it as a warm-season tender annual! Statice with its bright, showy flowers has become a main ingredient in our mixed bouquets.

You might be thinking that statice is not an interesting flower because it has been commonly used in commercial arrangements and grocery store bouquets for decades. But there's a reason it has been so popular with florists doing daily

home garden tip

When planting in an annual bed for display rather than cutting, spacing can be a bit wider, typically 12 inches (30 cm).

arrangements . . . it's a fabulous filler flower, very sturdy, and holds up like a dream!

- **Seeding and growing tips:** I found statice easy to start from seed and a strong grower in soil blocks. Statice likes its early growth to

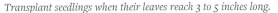

Transplant seedlings when their leaves reach 3 to 5 inches long.

occur in very cool temperatures. Fall planting is ideal, but if it will not survive winter temperatures in your area, plant as early as possible in that 6- to 8-week range before your last spring frost. Transplants have long flat leaves that grow mostly out instead of up, so we look for about 3 inches (7.5 cm) wide rather than tall to know when they're ready. Statice needs full sun to thrive, at least 12 to 13 hours per day of it for the best stem length and flower production. Shorter days (in the far northern or far southern hemispheres) will lengthen days to bloom. It produces many stems per plant from the base, so pinching is not required.

- **Flower support notes:** The base of this plant is low growing, but the strong flower stalks can get tall in the right conditions. Support is not required but may be beneficial in wind and rainstorms.

- **Harvesting and conditioning notes:** See Stage to harvest image (page 130). I harvest when most or all of the flowers in the cluster have opened and the white or yellow center is showing. In my experience, the flowers do not continue to open after cutting. Make the cut at the base of the stem and strip off any leaves. Follow the standard conditioning steps on page 32. Because statice stems are fleshy, they can harbor bacteria, so they benefit from water conditioning treatments (CVBN tablets, holding solution, and flower food). Statice is ethylene sensitive, which can cause early flower wilting but may not be very noticeable due to the papery nature of the flowers. If properly conditioned, expect fresh blooms to last 8 to 14 days in the vase. It can also be hung to dry in a warm, dark, well-ventilated room.

growing facts

Preferred season: Cool

Winter low temperature survival: 20°F (-7°C)

Starting from seed:
- Prefer to start seed indoors
- Start seed indoors 4 weeks before planting outdoors
- Prefer to start in ¾-inch (2 cm) soil blocks
- Prefers light to sprout; cover seeds lightly, under no more than ⅛ inch (0.3 cm) soil
- Soil temperature: 70°F or under (21°C)
- 7 to 14 days to sprout
- Air temperature for optimal transplant growth: 50 to 60°F (10 to 15.5°C)
- Transplant to the garden when: 3 inches (7.5 cm) wide (see following)

Sun requirement: Full sun

Height: 24 to 36 inches (60 to 90 cm)

Rows of plants per 36-inch (90 cm)-wide bed: 4

Plant spacing in row: 6 inches (15 cm)

Days to bloom: 110 to 120 days

Flower support: Not required

Fertilization: Standard bed preparation (see page 57); additional field applications may be beneficial

flower farmer insider tip

If you've never grown statice, consider starting with a color mix so you can see all the colors before you pick individual ones to grow. I particularly like the 'Seeker' rose shades, yellow, purple, and white for making bouquets.

- **Good to know:** Dried statice retains its color and is popular for use in dried flower wreaths as well as craft projects.

Favorite Varieties

'QIS Apricot' is a hybrid that grows tall and has this color that we can't get in the 'Seeker series'. It is so beautiful that we had to add it! Features blooms in apricot, peach, and coral tones; grows 30 inches (75 cm) tall.

'Seeker' series offer a mix, which we grow, as well as single colors as needed: blue, pastel blue, light yellow, purple, white, yellow, and rosy-pink shades. Produces 1½- to 3-inch (3.5 to 7.5 cm) flower clusters on strong stems; grows 30 inches (75 cm) tall.

RIGHT, FROM TOP *Stage to harvest: Allow the blooms to fully develop with all the little flowers open. Wilting may occur if harvested prematurely.*

Ready for fresh bouquets or to be dried: 'Seeker' mix including white, purple, blue, rose, and yellow with 'QIS Apricot' tucked in on the right side

Matthiola incana

Stock

Stock is an excellent cut flower with a spicy-sweet, clove-like scent. This flower became a key part of our spring bouquets and commercial sales once I finally figured out the proper timing of planting them in my garden! Their window of harvest is short for me, but perfectly timed during the high-demand season for cut flowers in early May. So, it is worth finding your correct planting timing.

- **Seeding and growing tips:** Stock prefers cool conditions from starting the seed to growing out in the garden and does not tolerate freezing. We plant seedlings out as early

flower farmer insider tip

You might have heard that flower farmers "select for doubleness" at the early seedling stage. It is true that most varieties of stock produce only about 50 to 60 percent double blooms, and that the double-blooming flowers are more in demand. However, the seedling selection process is time-consuming and hard to master. I have never practiced this and, instead, use the single bloom stems in our mixed bouquets.

Transplant when 3 to 5 inches tall and do not pinch because they only produce one flower per plant.

as possible in that 6- to 8-week range before our last spring frost. We row cover to protect from frost and cold wind. Because stock is a single-stem plant, it should never be pinched,

growing facts

Preferred season: Cool

Winter low temperature survival: 20°F (-7°C)

Starting from seed:
- Prefer to start seed indoors
- Start seed indoors 2 to 4 weeks before planting outdoors
- Prefer to start in ¾-inch (2 cm) soil blocks
- Needs light to sprout; cover seeds lightly, under no more than ⅛ inch (0.3 cm) soil
- Soil temperature: 60 to 68°F (15.5 to 20°C)
- 5 to 12 days to sprout
- Air temperature for optimal transplant growth: 60 to 65°F (15.5 to 18°C)
- Transplant to the garden when: 3 to 5 inches (7.5 to 13 cm) tall

Sun requirement: Full sun

Height: 24 to 36 inches (60 to 90 cm)

Rows of plants per 36-inch (90 cm)-wide bed: 9

Plant spacing in row: 6 inches (15 cm)

Days to bloom: 90 to 100

Flower support: Yes

Fertilization: Standard bed preparation (see page 57); additional field application may be beneficial (details following)

and we pack them close together to make the best use of space. Stock may benefit from a field application of fertilizer. If your summers are long and cool, consider planting several successions (every two weeks) of stock to harvest throughout the season.

- **Flower support notes:** If grown with nights in the range 50°F (10°C), stems should be strong enough that no additional support is needed. If grown in warmer overnight temperatures, as I do, softer stems are likely and need support.

- **Harvesting and conditioning notes:** See Stage to harvest image (page 133). I harvest when about half the flowers on the stalk have opened. Stock produces one flower per plant so you can choose where to make the harvest cut according to your need. Stock has no regrowth, unlike branching plants on which the harvest cut affects the regrowth. In my effort to get as much stem length as possible when harvesting, I cut at the base of the plant, sometimes down into the soil. If the end of the stem is woody, it could make the stem hard to hydrate and may be trimmed off. Follow the standard conditioning steps on page 32. Stock is a member of the "Dirty Dozen Flowers" (see page 33 for details). Stock flower tips will stretch and bend toward a light source, plus they lose fragrance over time. With that, plus the fact that they're extremely ethylene sensitive, it's best not to store them long. Stock does benefit from holding solution and flower food, allowing the top blooms to open and color up. If properly conditioned, expect fresh blooms to last 5 to 10 days in the vase. Stock can be hung to dry (pick when all flowers are open) in bunches of three to five stems in a warm

home garden tip

This sweet-smelling flower is definitely worth experimenting with to find the right time to plant in your garden!

place; if you do it quickly after harvesting, the flowers may retain some of their scent once dried.

- **Good to know:** Stock petals have a somewhat peppery flavor and are commonly used to accent salads, drinks, and desserts.

Favorite Varieties

'**Cheerful'** has been my best field-grown variety and is a hybrid that has a higher percentage of double blooms. It is offered in white and yellow; grows 24 to 36 inches (60 to 90 cm) tall.

'**Katz'** has a range of pastels and jewel tones, or you can grow a mix of the colors. They are typically 50 to 60 percent double blooms, with the 'Katz Hi Double White' having a higher rate of doubles; grows up to 30 inches (75 cm) tall.

RIGHT, FROM TOP *Stage to harvest: Cut as the first bottom blooms are opening. The head may still be growing and will continue to after harvest. 'Katz' apricot and yellow.*

Stock 'Iron' in peach, white, and rose grown by Wind Haven Farm.

Moluccella laevis

Bells of Ireland

Bells of Ireland brings a fabulously quirky look and a lovely green-apple scent to spring bouquets! The green bell shapes that cover the stems of this beauty are calyces with tiny white flowers in the center of each. Bells are deer resistant. They tend to do best in regions with long, cool summers. Even so, we were able to treat it as a flash crop to get a nice flush before our hot summer kicked in, and our customers were always grateful to have them!

- **Seeding and growing tips:** I store my cool-season hardy annual seeds in the freezer, but with bells, it is extra helpful to do this for at least 2 weeks before sowing to encourage stronger germination. After that, soak the seeds in water for a few hours before sowing to soften that hard outer seed coat to allow the seed embryo to break out. Do not cover the seed with soil. I direct seed in the garden in fall. If you are on the cusp of the winter low survival temperatures, it is worth experimenting with fall planting and using a floating row cover for added protection. If this flower will not survive your winter temperatures, see my special note in "Planting Seeds in the Garden" (page 48). Be sure to keep the seed bed moist during sprouting. I get excellent stem length and abundance on these well-established plants. Additional fertilization in the field is

beneficial after the soil has warmed in spring and new growth has restarted. Once the seedlings are about 5 inches (13 cm) tall, thin them to about one every 6 to 9 inches (15 to 23 cm) for cut flowers. Side shoots don't have time to mature for us before warm weather hits, so we don't pinch and, instead, cut one center stem bloom per plant. Bells can fall victim to diseases such as leaf spot or crown rot during rainy seasons. I have not found any way to prevent or treat these diseases when growing outdoors in the garden. In a good year, they are spectacular—that makes the years we lose them easier to accept.

BELOW, FROM LEFT *Seeds planted in the garden, shown from just sprouting to several weeks old.*

Stage to harvest: Cut when tall enough to be useful and before they develop thorns; I leave the leaves in between the bells.

growing facts

Preferred season: Cool

Winter low temperature survival: 10°F (-12°C)

Starting from seed:
- Prefer to sow directly in the field or garden
- Plant seeds 6 to 8 weeks before first fall frost
- Needs light to sprout; do not cover
- Soil temperature: 65°F (18°C)
- 14 to 21 days to sprout
- Air temperature for optimal growth: 60 to 65°F (15.5 to 18°C)

Sun requirement: Full sun, at least 6 to 8 hours

Height: 24 to 36 inches (60 to 90 cm)

Rows of plants per 36-inch (90 cm)-wide bed: 3

Plant spacing in row: 6 inches (15 cm)

Days to bloom: 90 to 110

Flower support: Yes

Fertilization: Standard bed preparation (see page 57); additional field applications may be beneficial

home garden tip

At the end of the season, leave a few flowers to mature so they will reseed the garden.

- **Flower support notes:** Netting is recommended. Due to the bell shape of the flowers, they tend to collect water and become heavy when it rains, so support netting keeps them upright. Because the plants are phototropic, they will bend upward to the light if they fall over, which makes them less usable for cuts.

- **Harvesting and conditioning notes:** See Stage to harvest image (page 135). The stems develop thorns as they mature, so harvest either before they develop or wear gloves

flower farmer insider tip

Because of the threat of disease, I begin harvesting as soon as the central stem is tall enough to be useful.

when cutting. Cut when half of the bells are open. Flowers continue to open after cutting. We harvest a single stem at ground level, but experiment with cutting above the bottom side shoots to see if they get long enough to harvest in your climate. This plant is not considered ethylene sensitive. Follow the standard conditioning steps on page 32. Bells benefit from the use of holding solution. With proper conditioning, expect fresh blooms to last 8 to 10 days in the vase.

- **Good to know:** Although I am always tempted to leave them in the garden for the stems to grow taller, experience has taught me to cut as soon as possible and use them. Bells are always in high demand!

Favorite Varieties

'Bells of Ireland' is how this seed is normally listed in catalogs, lacking a variety name. There is, on occasion, a shorter version available in nurseries called 'Pixie Bells', which may make a good landscape choice but will not grow tall enough for a cut flower.

Bells of Ireland naturally branch, and it makes them wonderful to use in bouquets. Their fragrance is one of my favorite spring smells.

Monarda hybrida
Hybrid Bee Balm

When I debuted a big handful of 'Lambada' on social media years ago, it created quite a stir. I was surprised how many of my flower-farming peers weren't familiar with it. I use it as a unique spring filler before those pinkish florets reveal themselves; the catch is learning how early you can harvest and prevent it from wilting!

'Lambada' looks like something out of a Dr. Seuss book, with the stem growing up through the pinkish-lavender blooms as they get smaller gradually toward the top. As a member of the bee balm family, the flowers are a favorite of pollinators and hummingbirds.

Although it is a cool-season hardy annual, this plant continues to thrive as the temperatures rise in summer. It's one of those flowers that

flower farmer insider tip

This flower is a good conversation starter at the farmers' market, particularly if not in bloom yet, and can be used as long-lasting foliage for bouquets that way. If you have florists who like "unusual" things, this is a great option to offer them.

may seem like a perennial but is mainly just a good reseeder in the garden or landscape. I have always grown it like an annual on my cut-flower farm, but I do discover it randomly growing where it has conveniently replanted itself.

Transplant to the garden when 3 to 5 inches tall.

growing facts

Preferred season: Cool

Winter low temperature survival: 10°F (-12°C)

Starting from seed:
- Prefer to start seed indoors
- Start seeds 4 to 6 weeks before planting outdoors
- Prefer to start in ¾-inch (2 cm) soil blocks
- Needs darkness to sprout; cover with soil
- Soil temperature: 70°F (21°C)
- 7 to 14 days to sprout
- Air temperature for optimal transplant growth: 70°F (21°C)
- Transplant to the garden when: 3 to 5 inches tall (7.5 to 13 cm)

Sun requirement: Full sun, at least 6 to 8 hours

Height: 24 to 36 inches (60 to 90 cm)

Rows of plants per 36-inch (90 cm)-wide bed: 4

Plant spacing in row: 6 inches (15 cm)

Days to bloom: 120

Flower support: Yes

Fertilization: Standard bed preparation (see page 57); additional field applications may be beneficial

- **Seeding and growing tips:** I find these quite easy to grow indoors from seed. We plant seedlings in fall for the following year's blooms, again in very early spring, and 4 weeks after that planting. I encourage growers where the climate might be just too cool for winter survival, to try planting in fall with row cover protection to get the earliest blooms. Plant 6 inches (15 cm) apart for cut flowers or 12 inches (30 cm) in the landscape. Field applications of fertilizer may be beneficial in the spring when the soil has warmed and new growth is seen. I like pinching 50 percent of the plants to help stagger the harvest; I do this either in the tray 7 to 14 days before planting or in the garden after they are established in either fall or spring once growing resumes. Those plants not pinched will bloom earlier, and after making that first deep harvest cut on the center stem, I find that the resulting branching also produces usable stems.

- **Flower support notes:** These tall stalks with heavy blooms benefit from flower support netting.

- **Harvesting and conditioning notes:** See Stage to harvest image (page 139). I like to harvest these right before they bloom, when the buds are a silvery green, but they can also be harvested as the blooms just start to turn color. Make the center stem cut near ground level, just above the lowest two or three side shoots. Make future cuts at the base of the stem being harvested, right at the branching point. If you have trouble with wilting, experiment with removing more of the lower foliage. The foliage may be fragrant. Follow the standard conditioning steps on page 32. These benefit from holding solution. Monarda is not known to be ethylene sensitive. Expect fresh blooms to last 8 to 10 days in the vase.

- **Good to know:** Monarda is also great for drying and is edible as well!

ABOVE, FROM LEFT *Stage to harvest: I harvest as the very first pink flower starts to show color.*

This unique flower and filler is also fragrant. This is one of our favorite early summer bouquet ingredients.

Favorite Varieties

'Lambada' is the pinkish-lavender flowering variety I grow because it grows tall and seems to be a little more resistant to powdery mildew than some other kinds of bee balm. Unlike other types of monarda, it is less likely to perennialize by developing runners that spread underground; however, it does reseed; grows 24 to 36 inches (60 to 90 cm).

home garden tip

To keep the blooms coming throughout the season, snip off fading blooms just above a leaf or branch. Leave a few stems to mature and reseed toward the end of the season. This is a great flower to attract bumblebees to your tomato plants.

Nigella damascena
Love-in-a-Mist

Love-in-a-mist has been popular in cottage gardens for a long time, and with good reason. Every aspect of these plants brings wonder and whimsy, whether growing in a garden bed or harvested for bouquets. The foliage is soft and fernlike, the blooms are finely detailed and exotic with delicate tendrils, and the oblong seedpods have a dramatic texturized look unlike any other we grow. They are deer resistant and good reseeders if the pods are allowed to fully develop in the garden or landscape.

Nigella has always been a significant part of our spring cutting garden because several of our florists would take all we had in fresh bloom or in newly developed seedpods. I learned through trial and error to harvest the seedpods early in their development to prevent blemishes and to prevent them from spilling their seeds onto tabletops from the vase.

- **Seeding and growing tips:** We always sow *Nigella* directly in the garden in fall. To get the tallest stems, even if you're on the cusp of their survivable winter lows, consider fall-planting them with a lightweight row cover. If this flower will not survive your winter temperatures, see my special note in "Planting Seeds in the Garden" (page 48). Fall-planted seedlings may benefit especially from additional fertilization in the field after the soil has warmed in spring and new growth has restarted. In spring, once the seedlings are about 5 inches (13 cm) tall, thin them with a hoe to about one every 6 inches

(15 cm). However, I tend to leave a bit closer spacing in my efforts to get taller stems with less branching and bigger flowers. We do not pinch as these are already short plants. Instead, the first center stem cut serves as the pinch, and side shoots may develop. *Nigella* will complete its growth cycle and start to fade as daytime temperatures reach 80°F (27°C).

- **Flower support notes:** Not needed

- **Harvesting and conditioning notes:** See Stage to harvest image (page 142). To use as a fresh-cut flower, cut when the main stem bloom has just begun to crack. Flowers

FROM LEFT *Nigella seed prefers to be planted in the garden, shown from just sprouting to several weeks old.*

From the center top and going around the circle: 'Delft Blue', 'Mrs. Jekyll' light blue, 'African Bride', 'Persian' mulberry rose, 'Midnight', 'Albion' green marbles, with a mix of their pods in the middle.

growing facts

Preferred season: Cool

Winter low temperature survival: 0°F (-18°C)

Starting from seed:
- Prefer to sow directly in the field or garden
- Plant seeds 6 to 8 weeks before first fall frost
- Needs darkness to sprout; cover lightly with soil
- Soil temperature: 60 to 65°F (15.5 to 18°C)
- 10 to 14 days to sprout
- Air temperature for optimal growth: 60 to 65°F (15.5 to 18°C)

Sun requirement: Full sun

Height: 18 to 24 inches (45 to 60 cm)

Rows of plants per 36-inch (90 cm)-wide bed: 3

Plant spacing in row: 6 inches (15 cm)

Days to bloom: 65 to 70 for flowers, 80 to 85 for seedpods

Flower support: Not needed

Fertilization: Standard bed preparation (see page 57); additional field applications may be beneficial

home garden tip

Nigella is great for containers as well as the garden bed. At the end of the season, leave a few flowers to form seedpods that will eventually reseed the garden for next year.

continue to open after cutting. Harvest the central stem almost at ground level, just above the lowest three or four side shoots. Future harvests can be made at the base of the stem. Follow the standard conditioning steps on page 32. It is not known to be ethylene sensitive. With proper conditioning, expect fresh blooms to last 7 to 10 days in the vase. To dry the seedpods, harvest them when fresh, and hang to dry.

- **Good to know:** There are some varieties sold by nurseries as bedding plants rather than for cut flowers, so be aware of the expected height of the variety you grow, and make sure it matches your intended use.

Favorite Varieties

'Albion' tends to grow taller with white blooms mixed with double or single rows of petals. The all-white flower of green marbles is followed by bright lime-green seedpods and

Stage to harvest: Cut as the bud is just cracking open until it develops its unique pod.

black marbles has dark plum-colored seedpods; grows to 24 inches (60 cm) tall.

'Mrs. Jekyll' produces lovely double blooms in shades of indigo blue, pink, white, and purple. The seedpods are green with purple stripes; grows to 20 inches (50 cm) tall.

flower farmer insider tip

The wide harvest window from fresh flower to seedpods makes this a very useful flower in our offerings. In my garden, *Nigella* was always a one-cut crop with little to no usable side shoots of harvesting quality. In cooler climates, you could experiment with planting both in fall and very early spring for two successions. Do not rely on reseeding for commercial crop production, as you will want to harvest all remaining seedpods for selling fresh and dried rather than leaving them in the field to fully develop.

Orlaya grandiflora

White Lace Flower

With delicate white lacy blooms and compact growth habits, *Orlaya* is a great fit for the cutting garden. Although it has a 2- to 3-inch umbel bloom form similar to *Ammi*, *Orlaya* has larger petals along the outer edges that give it a showier, more feminine look. We really love it as a bouquet filler paired with spring focal flowers.

I particularly love using the flower heads as they progress from a fresh bloom to developing seed. Not only do they add a unique texture to bouquets, but they last even longer as a cut flower at this stage. Keep your eye on the patch after the initial harvest of flowers for that period when all the petals have dropped and the remaining flower head reveals a beautifully textured green head. This stage may have a shorter window of harvest, but offers such a unique filler.

Orlaya is also well loved by early season pollinators and is deer resistant. Whenever space allows, I tend to leave these plants in my garden with their short side shoot flowers because of

home garden tip

At the end of the season, leave a few flowers to mature so they will reseed the garden for next year.

Orlaya seeds planted in the garden. Shown just emerging as skinny easy to miss seedlings alongside several weeks-old seedlings.

the flocks of beneficial insects and pollinators they attract. This flower is a strong reseeder in the landscape and works in containers, too!

- **Seeding and growing tips:** We sow white lace flowers directly into the garden in fall. Even if you're on the cusp of their survivable winter lows, consider fall planting them with a lightweight row cover. If this flower will not survive your winter temperatures, see my special note in "Planting Seeds in the Garden" (page 48). Fall-planted seedlings may benefit especially from additional fertilization in the field after the soil has warmed in spring and new growth has restarted. In spring, once the seedlings are 3 to 5 inches (7.5 to 13 cm) tall, thin them with a hoe to about one every 6 inches (15 cm) for cut flowers. We do not pinch as these are already short plants. Rather, we harvest by cutting flower stems very close to ground level to encourage additional long stems. To keep it blooming a little while longer as hot summer weather approaches (85°F [29°C] and above), consider planting where it will get mid- to late-afternoon shade.

- **Flower support notes:** I do not use flower support netting.

- **Harvesting and conditioning notes:** See Stage to harvest image (page 48). Cut when one-third of the tiny flowers are open. Flowers continue to open after cutting. Harvest just above ground level; future stems will emerge from the base. To improve hydration, strip off any side branches that have immature blooms on them. After cutting, allow to hydrate overnight before arranging or adding to a bouquet. It is unknown if *Orlaya* is ethylene sensitive. Follow the standard conditioning steps on page 32. With proper conditioning, expect fresh blooms to last 7 to 10 days in the vase. May also be cut for drying after seedpods have formed.

growing facts

Preferred season: Cool

Winter low temperature survival: -5°F (-20.5°C)

Starting from seed:
- Prefer to sow directly in the field or garden
- Plant seeds 6 to 8 weeks before first fall frost
- Needs light to sprout; do not cover
- Soil temperature: 60 to 65°F (15.5 to 18°C)
- 10 to 16 days to sprout
- Air temperature for optimal growth: 60 to 65°F (15.5 to 18°C)

Sun requirement: Full sun

Height: 24 inches (60 cm)

Rows of plants per 36-inch (90 cm)-wide bed: 3

Plant spacing in row: 6 inches (15 cm)

Days to bloom: 65 to 70

Flower support: Not needed

Fertilization: Standard bed preparation (see page 57); additional field applications may be beneficial

- **Good to know:** *Orlaya* is a member of the same *Daucus* family as Ammi, but it produces a smaller flower head that is easier to use in arrangements and is particularly popular for wedding work.

ABOVE, FROM LEFT *Stage to harvest: Cut when the blooms are just unfurling up through developing green seed heads yet pausing all harvesting during the shedding stage.*

Orlaya is a beauty and standout amongst similar looking spring flowers because of the outer layer of larger petals.

Favorite Varieties

'White Finch' has larger, broader outer petals than the more common strains and is showier. The fragrant lacy flowers are pure white; grows 28 inches (70 cm) tall.

'White Lace' has pure white blooms that are a little smaller than 'White Finch'; grows 28 inches (70 cm) tall.

flower farmer insider tip

The first flush of blooms will be the tallest; subsequent stems may be shorter as the season progresses. Fall planted *Orlaya* will produce the longest stems, but in areas with cooler summers, you may be able to extend your harvest with two or three very early spring successions spaced 2 weeks apart. Do not rely on reseeding for commercial crop production.

Papaver, Papaver nudicaule, Papaver somniferum

Iceland Poppy, Giant Poppy Pods

The delicate tissue-paper-like blooms of this family make poppies an all-time favorite both in a vase and the garden. As with sweet pea blossoms, the vase life of poppies can be shorter than other cut flowers, but they are some of the sweetest days with flowers in a vase! Growing poppies can seem hard because their lifecycle appears elusive and seeds can be difficult to sprout, but as with so many of these cool-season annuals, success lies in finding the right time to plant the right variety in your garden.

home garden tip

Plant poppies in a spot where you can allow them to reseed year after year, perhaps in a naturalized patch or roadside area.

There are both hardy annual and perennial types of poppies; I grow the hardy annuals as cut flowers. Some varieties may be more difficult to start from seed and to grow, whereas others just don't make good cut flowers.

My favorite poppy for fresh-cut flowers is the Iceland poppy 'Champagne Bubbles'. It's one of the earliest flowers to bloom on my farm. I have found success sowing the seeds directly in the garden and harvesting the blooms without special handling steps. For many gardeners, problems are common in both these areas. The turning point for me to succeed in growing full beds of poppies came when I learned to plant the seed more heavily. I also learned that taking a little more time to prepare the bed top for these seed gems was worth it.

- **Seeding and growing tips:** Direct sowing in the garden or field in late fall is recommended

ABOVE, FROM LEFT *Iceland poppy seedling sown in the garden. They often germinate in clusters, and I thin the clusters to 6 inches apart.*

Giant poppy pod seedlings just emerging; their seeds were planted in the garden. They are so thin and tiny they are easy to miss.

Stage to harvest: Cut Iceland poppies as soon as the bud begins to cracks and you can see the bloom color.

growing facts

Preferred season Cool

Winter low temperature survival: 0°F (-18°C)

Starting from seed:
- Prefer to direct sow in the garden
- Direct sow 6 to 8 weeks before first fall frost
- Needs light to sprout; do not cover
- Soil temperature: 70°F (21°C)
- 7 to 21 days to sprout
- Air temperature for optimal growth: 55 to 70°F (13 to 21°C)

Sun requirement: Full sun, minimum 8 hours, more is better

Height: Iceland, 12 to 30 inches (30 to 75 cm); pods, 36 to 60 inches (90 to 150 cm)

Rows of plants per 36-inch (90 cm)-wide bed: 4

Plant spacing in row: 6 inches (15 cm)

Days to bloom: 110 to 120 days, depending on variety and conditions

Flower support: See Flower Support Notes following

Fertilization: Standard bed preparation (see page 57)

if they survive your lowest winter temperatures. These seeds are tiny and should be sown on the soil surface and not covered with soil. I find creating a smooth and fine seed bed helps ensure the seed makes better contact with the soil. I follow the recommendations in "Planting Seeds in the Garden" (page 48) by creating shallow troughs with a hoe, seed heavily into the troughs, and then gently press down the row so the seeds make contact with the soil. I find that *P. somniferum* sprouts more quickly and with a higher rate of germination than *P. nudicaule*. With this in mind, I sow *P. nudicaule* more heavily. To sow either, I dump the tiny seeds into the palm of my hand. I deliberately only dump enough so they can scatter in my palm, making it easier and quicker to pick up just a couple of seeds at a time to drop every inch or so (see Cool-Season Tips, page 64). Seeds sown on the soil's surface need to be kept mois,t but be sure to water very gently so as not to wash out the seeds. Lightweight floating row cover can be placed to protect newly sown seeds from drying winds until seeds crack, but

flower farmer insider tip with
Bailey Hale, Ardelia Farm & Co.

CONDITIONING TIP

"Much is written about searing or burning the ends of poppies to seal in their milky sap. Alternatively, simply pick them and store dry in a closed cardboard box in your cooler. The stem will naturally seal itself. When you are ready to use the stems, simply stand them up in clean water in the cooler. They will start to open by the following morning. You can store dry flowers for up to a week with little decline in vase life."

lift it when watering. Poppies prefer daytime temps below 70°F (21°C) and nighttime temps below 60°F (15.5°C) and will stop performing once temps go above that for the season. Because poppies can be slow to sprout, be sure to keep up on weed prevention in the bed; see "Weed Prevention in the Garden When Planting Seeds" (page 41). In early spring, thin to 6-inch (15 cm) spacing. Pinching is not required because all stems sprout from the base of the plant. If fall-planted, poppies may benefit from light fertilization in spring after growth has restarted.

- **Flower support notes:** I use flower support netting on *P. somniferum* plantings because the tall stems are susceptible to wind and rain as they go through the blooming to pod development stages. I do not use support

netting on *P. nudicaule* plantings because they are much shorter and are harvested in bud stage, eliminating most of the risk of stems toppling over in the garden.

- **Harvesting and conditioning notes:** See Stage to harvest image (page 147). *P. nudicaule* should be harvested just as the fuzzy outer sheath starts to crack and the flower bud's color is visible. You may need to harvest more than once per day during their peak. Cut at the base of the stem near ground level and other stems will emerge from the bushy base of the plant. Expect blooms to open quickly once cut. Storage of cut stems is not recommended because the thin stems and petals are easily damaged, but storing for as much as a week in a cooler is unlikely to affect vase life. They benefit greatly from the use of holding solution. Blooms cut at the proper stage typically last 5 to 7 days in the vase. *P. somniferum* can be harvested when the desired pod size is reached and used either fresh (with a similar vase life) or hung to dry. The pods have a wide window of harvest for fresh use, keeping in mind that the light green pods can become soiled by insects, making them less desirable. I like to harvest the pods fairly early, at the size of a golf ball, for mixed bouquet uses and leave a small portion to grow on and swell to their name's sake 'Giant' for those commercial customers who want them, and also to save seed.

- **Good to know:** Poppies announce spring for me, and I love harvesting handfuls of this productive plant to make big bouquets of just their beautiful blooms.

Favorite Varieties

PAPAVER NUDICAULE

'Champagne Bubbles' is an Iceland poppy variety that features bushy plants with strong stems and beautiful 2- to 3-inch (5 to 7.5 cm) crepe paper–like blooms. In ideal conditions, expect as many as ten to fifteen flowering stems per plant. If thriving where planted, they'll likely

FROM LEFT *Save the seeds of P. somniferum: Allow the pods to dry in the garden and crack them open for the next season's seeds.*

Giant poppy pods have a bloom that only last about 24 hours. It is the green pods that are revealed when the petals fall off that we sold fresh or dried to save seed.

Iceland Poppy 'Champagne Bubbles'

flower farmer insider tip

I have ordered plugs of *Papaver nudicaule* when needed, and they perform beautifully. Consider buying plugs if you struggle with direct sowing; they can be planted out in fall or very early spring. The relatively short vase life of Iceland poppies makes them better suited for event work rather than for inclusion in a mixed bouquet subscription. However, 'Giant Poppy Pods' can be used at any size or stage of seedpod development and are desirable to florists in a broad range of sizes as well as dried, and they are a great mixed bouquet ingredient.

reseed themselves for the following year. It blooms in red, pink, orange, white, peach, and yellow with yellowish-green centers; grows 12 to 20 (30 to 50 cm) tall.

'Hummingbird' also known as 'Colibri', is another variety of Iceland poppy. Although this variety grows taller and produces larger buds and blooms than 'Champagne Bubbles', I find them a risky crop to grow outdoors. I grew this beautiful mix in my garden for three seasons. I had great success that first year, as we experienced a dry and cool spring. My second and third seasons turned out to be rainy springs, which led many of those big buds to rot before they could even open. I started from seed for two of those seasons and ordered plugs once. Blooms in white, yellow, orange, pink, and peach; grows 20 to 30 inches (50 to 75 cm) tall.

PAPAVER SOMNIFERUM

'Giant Poppy Pods' is a variety grown for the large seedpods it produces after flowering. The flowers, though, while lovely, are very short-lived, lasting little more than a couple of days and so are not suitable for cutting. The seedpods are very popular with florists, both in their fresh green state and also dried. This variety is slightly more heat tolerant than *P. nudicaule* and blooms later. Pods can be harvested into early summer, but the poppies will eventually stop flowering. This variety produces a very high volume of viable seed, so if left in the garden, it will very likely reseed itself year after year. Blooms are red-pink and large; grows 36 to 60 inches (90 to 150 cm) tall.

Rudbeckia, Rudbeckia hirta (annual), *Rudbeckia triloba* (short-lived perennial)

Black-Eyed Susan

The *Rudbeckia* family plays a significant role on my flower farm as a cut-flower crop. This family has a variety of lifecycles, including annuals, biennials, and perennials. So, it can be confusing to figure out when and where to plant them in order to have easy and productive garden plants. After growing and selling tons of *Rudbeckia* stems, I've learned it all comes down to identifying the habit of a variety, planting it in the right spot at the right time, and the rest is smooth sailing.

A wonderful residual benefit of this family of flowers became apparent as I began growing more and more varieties. I watched as my farm came alive with native bees and birds. With the beautiful blooms already being in high demand as a commercial crop and bouquet ingredient, I decided to allow those with a stronger reseeding nature to create habitat islands adjacent to my cutting gardens. These permanent reseeding islands are anchored with *R. triloba*, but also host other native plantings. They have become

home base to many insect-eating native birds, turtles, frogs, and other beneficial creatures— and they supply endless cut flowers. Instead of being annoyed with the habit of some of these strong reseeder varieties, I have learned how to best fit them into my garden plan. To control and prevent reseeding, plant fewer plants and harvest all the blooms all season to prevent the plants from developing and scattering seed.

How I Helped Rudbeckia *Fit into My Garden*

Rudbeckia hirta: This flower is technically a very short-lived perennial that I grow as an annual. Some are reseeders as noted in the Favorite Varieties (following), but I do not rely on reseeding for production. *R. hirta* does not require a cold period to bloom so it can be

Transplant seedlings to the garden when the leaves reach 3 to 5 inches.

flower farmer insider tip

To ensure a reliable harvest of this significant crop and for the easiest weed prevention practices, I plant new seedlings each year. If it survives your winter, *Rudbeckia* is best planted in fall, resulting in the most robust plants with the longest stems. The seed cones can also be sold without petals, either fresh or dried. Because these flowers are long lasting, they have become a key ingredient in our mixed bouquets.

succession planted, but plants do require 12 hours of day length to initiate flowering, so plan your successions accordingly. If they can survive your winter low temperatures, fall plantings provide the tallest and most abundance of

growing facts

Preferred season: Cool

Winter low temperature survival: -20°F (-29°C)

Starting from seed:
- Prefer to start seed indoors
- Start seed indoors 6 to 8 weeks before planting outdoors
- Prefer to start in ¾-inch (2 cm) soil blocks
- Needs light to sprout; do not cover
- Soil temperature: 70°F (21°C)
- 7 to 14 days to sprout
- Air temperature for optimal transplant growth: 60 to 75°F (15.5 to 24°C)
- Transplant to the garden when: 3 to 5 inches (7.5 to 13 cm) tall

Sun requirement: Full sun

Height: 18 to 48 inches (45 to 120 cm), depending on variety and conditions

Rows of plants per 36-inch (90 cm)-wide bed: 4

Plant spacing in row: 6 inches (15 cm)

Days to bloom: 90 to 120 days, depending on variety and season

Flower support: Yes

Fertilization: Standard bed preparation (see page 57); additional field applications may be beneficial seasonally

stems. I plant in fall, very early spring, and in spring for later blooms. In recent years, several hybridized varieties have been brought to market that greatly expand the color palette.

Rudbeckia triloba: This short-lived perennial has an aggressive reseeding habit I embrace and provide space for. When growing in an annual cutting garden, plant in fall or very early spring for late-summer spray-like stems with smallish blooms. I have not found succession planting to be successful.

- **Seeding and growing tips:** *Rudbeckia* is a relatively slow-sprouting and growing transplant, so these plants should be started on the earlier side of your ideal planting window. Sow seeds firmly on the surface of the soil blocks. Place on a wire cooling rack set on top of a heat mat. Newly sown seeds need to be kept moist, so I lay wide-weave burlap over the blocks until the seeds start to crack. Pinching is not necessary since flower stems emerge from the base of the plant. Once established, it is relatively low maintenance and drought tolerant.

- **Flower support notes:** I use flower support netting on all cutting garden plantings; I do not use it in naturalized areas. Although the base of these plants (clumps of leafy greens) rarely grows taller than 12 inches (30 cm), the flower stems shoot up much taller. The stems are typically sturdy but can still go down in wind and rain.

- **Harvesting and conditioning notes:** See Stage to harvest image (page 153). Harvest very low on the stem, about 2 to 3 inches (5 to 7.5 cm) from the base, as additional stems emerge from the base. Depending on the pest pressure I am experiencing, I have a wide range of harvest stages. When pests are causing damage, I begin harvesting when petals are just starting to lift off the flower face. This protects the flowers from chewing and staining pest damage. I harvest later in development when possible. Double-bloom varieties may need to develop in the field slightly longer before cutting. *Rudbeckia* benefits from traditional conditioning steps including chlorine tablets and holding solution and may hydrate better when cut early in the morning. When forced to harvest early in development due to pests, 2 tablespoons

BELOW, CLOCKWISE FROM TOP LEFT *Stage to harvest: Rudbeckias can be harvested while the bloom is opening to prevent pest damage or left to continue developing. Left to right: 'Denver Daisy', 'Prairie Sun', 'Cherokee Sunset', 'Maya', and 'Goldilocks'.*

Rudbeckias are great for the cutting garden and the landscape. This family of plants is a favorite of native bees.

'Indian Summer' is one of those first flowers I grew as a flower farmer. I was hooked by their giant blooms and tall abundant stems.

'Sahara' has some of the prettiest bicolor blooms that include buttercream and some yellow.

(30 ml) of hydrating solution in the harvest bucket can help prevent wilting. *Rudbeckia* is not ethylene sensitive (see "Cut-Flower Stem Care," page 30). Blooms are long lasting in the vase, typically 7 to 14 days.

- **Good to know:** On occasion, for undetermined reasons, a random *Rudbeckia* stem, most often the 'Indian Summer' variety, will wilt a couple of days after harvest. Researchers have not been able to determine what causes this phenomenon. I rarely experience this but mention it as it does occur.

'Prairie Sun' is a favorite for making bouquets. It's green-eyed, nice size blooms, and lighter yellow make it a neutral that fits all color schemes.

Favorite Varieties

RUDBECKIA HIRTA

'Cherokee Sunset' produces such amazing variations or color, with 4- to 5-inch (10 to 13 cm) mostly double blooms in a range of sunset tones, including golden yellow, rusty orange, chocolatey bronze, and some lovely bicolor combinations. It is a poor reseeder in my garden; grows 24 to 48 inches (60 to 120 cm) tall.

'Cherry Brandy' has become another surprise favorite! The blooms produce a compact plant with beautiful 3- to 4-inch (7.5 to 10 cm) dark cherry blooms. It is a poor reseeder in my garden; grows 20 to 30 inches (50 to 75 cm) tall.

'**Denver Daisy**' is a new surprise favorite of ours! The large 4- to 7-inch (10 to 18 cm) bicolor blooms are a deep, rusty chocolate with golden tips. It is a poor reseeder in my garden; grows 24 to 32 inches (60 to 80 cm) tall.

'**Double Daisy**' produces large 4- to 5-inch (10 to 13 cm) beautiful long-lasting golden-yellow blooms with several rows of petals. I love harvesting this one early, before the petals unfurl, for the texture it adds to bouquets. A strong reseeder. The stem length varies a bit more; it can be 24 to 48 inches (60 to 120 cm) tall.

'**Goldilocks**' produces 3- to 4-inch (7.5 to 10 cm) orangey-yellow semidouble blooms that are the earliest to bloom in our garden when fall-planted. These blooms are great fun to grow because they often suffer from a disorder called "fasciation." Scientists aren't sure what causes it, but our customers love the deformed flat blooms that result. An occasional reseeder; grows 24 to 36 inches (60 to 90 cm) tall.

'**Indian Summer**' is the largest variety we grow, with 4- to 7-inch (10 to 18 cm) blooms with golden-yellow petals and a chocolate brown eye. This one has been around a long time (it was the Association of Specialty Cut Flower Growers' 2000 Fresh Cut Flower of the Year). It is easy to grow and has a long vase life. One of the stronger reseeders; grows 36 to 48 inches (90 to 120 cm) tall.

'**Maya**' is a unique dwarf plant with frilly, fully double 4-inch (10 cm) blooms in golden yellow. Fall planting produces the tallest stem lengths. Poor reseeder; grows 18 to 24 inches (45 to 60 cm) tall.

home garden tip

Rudbeckia is a great addition to a natural "wildflower"-type landscape planting, or even as a mass stand of flowers along a driveway or roadside. Encourage reseeding by leaving flowers to develop seeds to self-scatter. It can be fun to see what blooms next season.

'**Prairie Sun**' features bicolor yellow petals with a green eye—quite a stunner! It is one of my favorites for bouquets because its color fits all and the blooms are a perfect 3- to 4-inch (7.5 to 10 cm) size. Poor reseeding habit; grows 24 to 36 inches (60 to 90 cm) tall.

'**Sahara**' offers a beautiful mix of 2- to 3 ½-inch (5 to 8.5 cm) copper, yellow, and brown-tone flowers with a brown eye. It is a poor reseeder in my garden. A more compact grower than some of the others at 24 to 36 inches (60 to 90 cm) tall.

RUDBECKIA TRILOBA
'**Triloba**' is our favorite late-season bloomer, featuring tall sturdy stems with branching sprays of small (1- to 1 ½-inch [2.5 to 3.5 cm]) yellow-petaled blooms on each stem. An excellent late-summer bouquet filler. A plant may live more than one season, but its aggressive reseeding is what keeps us knee deep in stems. This is a strong grower for us, which has naturalized and incorporated into the native border surrounding the farm. I have experienced some interesting variation in the stem structure with this variety, some with a more open spread between blooms and the other a tighter close-together habit; grows 36 to 72 inches (90 to 180 cm) tall.

Saponaria vaccaria hispanica

Soapwort, Cow Soapwort, Cow Herb, Cow Cockle

Saponaria is a new flower discovery for me. I only learned about it in the past decade. I was visiting with a flower-farmer friend, and he casually asked me if I planted my *Saponaria* in the fall or early spring. Much to his surprise, my reply was that I had never grown it! That following season, I sowed my first seeds in the garden and have never looked back.

Soapwort has long been loved as a cottage garden plant, with dainty blooms dancing atop blue-gray stems and foliage in airy sprays. The butterflies and moths adore it,

Saponaria seeds are easy to sprout in the garden and their preferred way to start. Shown 5 weeks after planting and before thinning that I normally do in very early spring.

as they are its natural pollinators. It makes for a wonderful filler flower for spring bouquets, often blooming just in time for Mother's Day. When spring comes, I always find myself wondering why I didn't plant more of this flower. Because of its ease of use in such high-demand seasonal colors, I find that my commercial customers love it as much as I do.

- **Seeding and growing tips:** Although soapwort thrives in areas with cooler summers, I grow it successfully as a spring flash crop on my farm when I plant in fall as a cool-season hardy annual. If this flower will not survive your winter temperatures, see my special note in "Planting Seeds in the Garden" (page 48).

growing facts

Preferred season: Cool

Winter low temperature survival:
10°F (-12°C)

Starting from seed:
- Prefer to sow directly in the field or garden
- Plant seeds 6 to 8 weeks before first fall frost
- Needs light to sprout; cover very lightly with soil, no more than ⅛ inch (0.3 cm)
- Soil temperature: 70°F (21°C)
- 7 to 10 days to sprout

Sun requirement: Full sun

Height: 24 to 36 inches (60 to 90 cm)

Rows of plants per 36-inch (90 cm)-wide bed: 3

Plant spacing in row: 6 inches (15 cm)

Days to bloom: 55 to 65

Flower support: Optional

Fertilization: Standard bed preparation (see page 57); additional field applications may be beneficial

home garden tip

Leave a few flower heads on the plants in the garden to encourage reseeding. Although perennial varieties of soapwort can be prolific spreaders, the annual variety that I grow is more well-behaved in a mixed planting.

Stage to harvest: Cut when a third of the small flowers on a stem are open. This bunch was grown by the End of Nowhere Flower Farm, Suffolk, VA.

If you're in a region with cooler summers, you may be able to direct sow seeds weeks before your last spring frost, and even succession plant every 2 to 3 weeks into midsummer. Soapwort likes well-drained soil, so raised beds are ideal. I plant three rows per bed and weed them periodically with my standing hoe. Fall-planted seedlings may benefit from additional fertilization in the field after the soil has warmed in spring and new growth has started. In early spring when growth starts back up (or for spring-planted seedlings when they show two or three sets of true leaves), I weed again and thin the rows to one plant every 6 inches (15 cm) or so. Pinching is not required as the plant is naturally branching. Multiple stems emerge from the base of the plant.

- **Flower support notes:** Because this plant is quick to mature and has an airy, open branching habit with sprays of smaller flowers, netting is not mandatory. However, netting may keep the plants a bit tidier, especially if you have wet springs.

flower farmer insider tip

Typically, a single stem is all you need to add a soft, airy feel to spring bouquets. I find the white variety particularly useful as a bouquet filler, but the pink can be a sweet addition, too, depending on the other colors in your spring lineup.

- **Harvesting and conditioning notes:** See Stage to harvest image (page 157). Harvest just as the first flowers on a stem start to crack open. Flowers continue to open after cutting. Make the cut at ground level. For best hydration, strip off all lower leaves and branches. Follow the standard conditioning steps on page 32. Use of holding solution is recommended. This flower may be ethylene sensitive. With proper water conditioning, expect blooms to last 5 to 7 days in the vase.

- **Good to know:** Soapwort gets its name from the saponin chemical naturally occurring in the leaves, which forms the bubbles in soap. To make your own liquid soap, boil 1 cup (about 55 g) of soapwort leaves in 2 cups (480 ml) of water for 30 minutes, then cool and strain. Note that this soap only keeps for about a week and that some people's skin may be sensitive to it.

Favorite Varieties

'Beauty' series produces an airy spray of 1-inch (2.5 cm) blossoms on tall stems, offered in both pink and white; grows 24 to 36 inches (60 to 90 cm) tall.

'Beauty' in pink and white is such a welcome spring bouquet ingredient. They are a little smaller than cosmos but give that same light and airy effect.

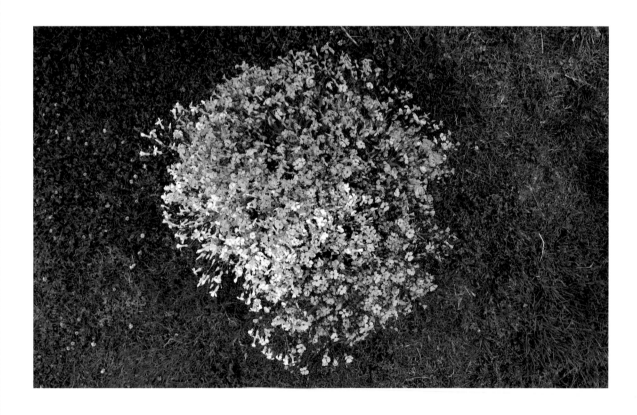

Scabiosa, Scabiosa atropurpurea, Scabiosa stellata

Pincushion Flower, Scabiosa Pincushion 'Ping Pong', Starflower

With a light honey scent, *Scabiosa* is well-loved by bumblebees and is a plant that offers uniqueness to bouquets during all of its life stages. The annual varieties we grow are different from the perennial varieties that you might find for sale at a local nursery and are commonly called pincushion flowers for the more pronounced rounded fluffy shape of their flower head.

- **Seeding and growing tips:** Even though this plant will survive our winter lows, we find that using a lightweight row cover gives them the "winter jacket" that really helps them thrive. Though considered a cool-season hardy annual, you may find that the plants may continue to bloom through your summer as well. Because they can live a little longer into summer, additional fertilization in the field will likely be beneficial. Pinching is not required as new stems emerge from the base of the plant and each plant will produce several stems.

- **Flower support notes:** *Scabiosa* have somewhat thin, wiry stems, so they benefit from support netting, particularly in wind and rain.

- **Harvesting and conditioning notes:** See Stage to harvest image (page 161), and the special harvesting note in the description for 'Ping Pong'. Stems bear single button-like buds that start to show color before they bloom. They can be cut and used starting at that stage and after, up to when one-third of the tiny flowers have opened. Flowers continue to open

ABOVE, FROM TOP *Top left and around the circle: 'Fata Morgan', 'QIS white', 'Fire King', 'Blue Cockadee', and 'Black Knight'.*

Transplant to the garden when 3 to 5 inches tall.

home garden tip

At the end of the season, leave a few flowers to mature and reseed the garden for next year.

after cutting. Harvest the central stem almost at ground level, just above the lowest three to four side shoots. Future harvests can be made at the base of the stem. Follow the standard

growing facts

Preferred season: Cool

Winter low temperature survival: 10°F (-12°C)

Starting from seed:
- Prefer to start seed indoors
- Start seed indoors 4 to 6 weeks before planting outdoors
- Prefer to start in ¾-inch (2 cm) soil blocks
- Needs some light to sprout; cover only very lightly with soil
- Soil temperature: 65 to 70°F (18 to 21°C)
- 10 to 14 days to sprout
- Air temperature for optimal transplant growth: 50 to 55°F (10 to 13°C)
- Transplant to the garden when: 3 to 5 inches (7.5 to 13 cm) tall

Sun requirement: Full sun, at least 6 to 8 hours

Height: 24 to 48 inches (60 to 120 cm)

Rows of plants per 36-inch (90 cm)-wide bed: 4

Plant spacing in row: 6 inches (15 cm)

Days to bloom: 90 to 100

Flower support: Yes

Fertilization: Standard bed preparation (see page 57); additional field applications may be beneficial

conditioning steps on page 32. I leave a couple of the side buds on these stems and find them easy to hydrate without wilting. This flower is not known to be ethylene sensitive. With proper conditioning, expect blooms to last 7 to 10 days in the vase.

- **Good to know:** *Scabiosa* planted near tomatoes will increase fruit yields because they attract bumblebees, which are primary pollinators for tomatoes.

Favorite Varieties

SCABIOSA ATROPURPUREA

'**Black Knight**' is a very deep burgundy, which looks nice as an accent or contrast color when mixed with some of the brighter blooms of spring and summer; grows 24 to 48 inches (60 to 120 cm) tall.

'**Blue Cockade**' is a bluish lavender color. This has been a career-long favorite color for commercial customers and for our bouquets; grows 24 to 48 inches (60 to 120 cm) tall.

'**Fata Morgana**' offers a range of creamy yellow to blush pink hues, which is extra beautiful for wedding work. I find it best to harvest this variety early in the developing stage, as the color fades quickly; grows 24 to 48 inches (60 to 120 cm) tall.

'**Fire King**' is a brighter, lighter red—sort of a berry tone; grows 24 to 48 inches (60 to 120 cm) tall.

'**QIS™ White**' with its lime-green buds and soft white blooms, this one goes with everything! I tend to harvest it early to use in the green-white stage as it will quickly appear dirty as it ages; grows 24 to 48 inches (60 to 120 cm) tall.

SCABIOSA STELLATA

'Ping Pong' is unique for its seedpod rather than the flower. As the cream and pale-blue blossoms fade, the lovely 2-inch (5 cm) round pod develops with honeycomb-shaped segments and a little black star in the center of each. Harvest just as those stars are turning black for the best quality pod to use fresh or dried; grows 24 to 36 inches (60 to 90 cm) tall.

flower farmer insider tip

Depending on your climate, you might be able to extend the harvest with additional successions plantings 2 to 4 weeks after the very early spring planting. In my garden, I fall and very early spring plant and follow up the latter with one more, 4 weeks later.

Stage to harvest: Cut S. atropurpurea in the button stage and until a third of the small flowers are opening. Cut S. stellata after the flower has faded and the pod has developed.

Tanacetum parthenium, a.k.a. *Chrysanthemum parthenium*,
a.k.a. *Pyrethrum parthenium*

Feverfew, Matricaria

The name "feverfew" comes from the Latin word for "fever reducer." Early Greek physicians prescribed it for fevers and as an inflammatory. One thing is for sure, it can cure your summer filler flower needs! These adorable clusters of tiny white flowers are so useful and coordinate with all other colors. Plus they are deer resistant!

- **Seeding and growing tips:** Feverfew is quite winter hardy. If it survives your lowest winter temperatures, I encourage you to plant it in fall. Even if you're on the cusp of its survival winter temperature range, consider experimenting with planting it in fall, using a lightweight floating row cover for protection. Because feverfew blooms when daylight hours are extended, succession planting may not be as beneficial as for other flowers because they all tend to bloom around the same time in summer. With shorter days, they will still bloom but will take longer and

Transplant to the garden when 3 to 5 inches tall.

growing facts

Preferred season: Cool

Winter low temperature survival: -10°F (-23°C)

Starting from seed:
- Prefer to start seed indoors
- Start seed indoors 4 to 6 weeks before planting outdoors
- Prefer to start in ¾-inch (2 cm) soil blocks
- Needs light to sprout; do not cover
- Soil temperature: 70°F (21°C)
- 7 to 14 days to sprout
- Air temperature for optimal transplant growth: 35 to 50°F (2 to 10°C)
- Transplant to the garden when: 3 to 5 inches (7.5 to 13 cm) tall

Sun requirement: Full sun

Height: 30 to 48 inches (75 to 120 cm)

Rows of plants per 36-inch (90 cm)-wide bed: 4

Plant spacing in row: 6 to 12 inches (15 to 30 cm)

Days to bloom: 100 to 110 days

Flower support: Yes

Fertilization: Standard bed preparation (see page 57); additional field applications may be beneficial

have shorter stems. This could be beneficial, and I encourage experimenting for your conditions and needs. Fall-planted seedlings may benefit especially from additional fertilization in the field after the soil has warmed in spring and new growth has restarted.

- **Flower support notes:** Feverfew can get quite tall and benefits from support netting to protect it from rain and windstorms.

- **Harvesting and conditioning notes:** See Stage to harvest image (above). Depending on your desired use, feverfew can be harvested at any stage, from buds just forming to blooms fully open. Flowers do not continue to open after cutting. Harvest the central stem almost at ground level, just above the lowest three or four side shoots. Future harvests can be made at the base of the stem. For best hydration, strip off all lower leaves and branches. Only what you'll see at the top of the bouquet or arrangement should remain. It is not known to be ethylene sensitive. Follow the standard

Stage to harvest: The button-type varieties like on the left can be cut when ⅓ of the blooms are open. Allow 'Vegmo Single' (on the right) and 'Tetra White Wonder' to almost completely open before harvesting.

conditioning steps on page 32. Feverfew is a member of the "Dirty Dozen Flowers" (see page 33 for details). With proper water conditioning, expect fresh blooms to last about 7 days in the vase.

- **Good to know:** In my book *Cool Flowers*, I state that feverfew repels insects, but in years since I have had a different experience. In my garden, I notice that it has many insect visitors. It may be considered invasive in areas where it grows as a short-lived perennial.

home garden tip

Leave a few flower heads intact at the end of the season to mature and produce seeds for next year's garden.

Favorite Varieties

'Tetra White Wonder' is a vigorous grower with fully double blooms forming an airy look, almost like a floating cloud. Blooms are white with a citrusy lemon-lime center; grows to 48 inches (120 cm) tall.

'Vegmo' series my all-time favorite, 'Single', in this variety has little white button-like flowers with yellow centers that look like a bunch of tiny daisies and are so cute in bouquets! We also grow the 'Vegmo Yellow', 'Sunny Ball', and 'Snowball Extra' varieties, because each has a little bit different coloring and bloom shape; grows to 48 inches (120 cm) tall.

'Virgo' is a stockier, sturdier plant, a slightly shorter variety but with nice, straight stems. The blooms are clustered more at the top of the plant (branching occurs more toward the top of the stems, so it's less airy looking). Attractive white blooms with yellow centers; grows to 36 inches (90 cm) tall.

flower farmer insider tip

Feverfew may be considered a short-lived perennial in some climates, but in our area, it's mostly a prolific reseeder, not growing back from the same root system as the previous year. Although reseeding is nice, it's not predictable and often doesn't stay in the row/bed, so we just can't rely on it for commercial production. Treat your feverfew crop like a hardy annual so you'll always have a good harvest.

Top left: 'Virgo', 'Vegmo' snowball extra, 'Vegmo single', 'Tetra White Wonder', and 'Vegmo' yellow

Trachelium caeruleum

Throatwort, Blue Throatwort, Throat Flower

This is a beautiful plant with an unfortunate name! Once thought to treat throat maladies, its real talent is adding a striking violet-purple flat-topped cluster of tiny star-shaped blooms to your garden or your spring cut-flower lineup. This flower is a great accent to some of the showier focal blooms you may have. *Trachelium* attracts bees, butterflies, and hummingbirds but not deer—so that's good news for gardeners!

Trachelium is native to the Mediterranean in places such as Morocco, Portugal, and Spain where the temperate climates are on the drier side. There, and in similar climates on the

home garden tip

Remove faded blooms regularly to encourage additional blooming, then leave a few blooms on the plants to fully mature and encourage reseeding.

Transplant to the garden when they reach 3 to 5 inches tall. They are slow-growing transplants.

West Coast of the United States, it grows as a short-lived perennial, spreading gradually from reseeding. In most other places, it can only be grown as an annual. And in places with hot summers, like mine, I grow it as a fall-planted cool-season hardy annual.

- **Seeding and growing tips:** *Trachelium* seeds are very tiny, so they're most often sold pelleted rather than raw to make them easier to handle and plant. Light aids germination, so sow seeds firmly on the top of the soil blocks. They're ready to plant out when the leaves reach 3 inches (7.5 cm) tall or wide (or are big enough to handle), spaced 6 inches (15 cm) apart for cut flowers or 12 inches (30 cm) in the garden.

  In places with hot summers, consider planting where they'll get mid- to late-

BELOW, FROM LEFT *Stage to harvest: Cut when a third of the tiny flowers are opening.*

The 'Lake Michigan' mix produces stems are good size, strong and stiff, plus love the foliage and the bloom colors.

flower farmer insider tip

Trachelium plugs are available commercially, which might be helpful for those who are too busy to give the extra care seedlings need in late summer/ early fall before planting out. Like lisianthus, they require consistent indoor growing conditions and can be slow growers. So, to ensure I have good quality seedlings to plant, I often order plugs.

afternoon shade. I find *Trachelium* to be extremely winter hardy on my farm, even without row cover protection, but you may want to offer it, depending on your conditions. Our warm summers really do them in; they prefer daytime temperatures of 70 to 75°F (21 to 24°C) maximum. Growers in warm climates may do best growing this one over winter if day lengths are long enough. Fall-planted seedlings may benefit from an additional application of fertilizer (for nitrogen) when soil has warmed

and growth has restarted in spring, but discontinue fertilizer one month before blooming. *Trachelium* will begin flowering in summer when day length stretches past 14 hours. Stems emerge from the plant base, so pinching is not required. Expect three to four stems per plant.

- **Flower support notes:** Because these are top-heavy blooms on tall stems, they benefit from flower support netting.

- **Harvesting and conditioning notes:** See Stage to harvest image (page 167). Harvest when about one-third of the tiny florets on the main umbel are blooming, making the cut at ground level. If harvested much earlier than that, the flowers might not continue to open. Follow the standard conditioning steps on page 32. Cut stems benefit from use of holding solution. *Trachelium* is ethylene sensitive, which may cause the tiny florets to stop opening or even close. Expect fresh blooms to last 10 to 14 days in the vase. This plant can be air-dried, but the blooms lose most of their color.

- **Good to know:** As with many white flowers, the florets of the white *Trachelium* tend to age more rapidly than their darker counterparts. Experiment with how early you can cut the white ones and still have the florets continue to open.

growing facts

Preferred season: Cool

Winter low temperature survival: 20°F (-7°C)

Starting from seed:
- Prefer to start seed indoors
- Start seeds 6 to 8 weeks before planting outdoors
- Prefer to start in ¾-inch (2 cm) soil blocks
- Needs light to sprout; do not cover with soil
- Soil temperature: 70°F (21°C)
- 7 to 14 days to sprout
- Air temperature for optimal transplant growth: 55 to 60°F (13 to 15.5°C)
- Transplant to the garden when: 3 to 5 inches (7.5 to 13 cm) tall

Sun requirement: Full to part sun, 4 to 8 hours

Height: 24 to 30 inches (60 to 75 cm)

Rows of plants per 36-inch (90 cm)-wide bed: 4

Plant spacing in row: 6 inches (15 cm)

Days to bloom: 112 to 140

Flower support: Yes

Fertilization: Standard bed preparation (see page 57); additional field application may be beneficial

Favorite Varieties

'Lake Michigan' series offers large center stem blooms 3 to 6 inches (7.5 to 15 cm) across on tall stems, with smaller umbels on the side branches. This variety tends to bloom in late spring/early summer. My favorite colors to grow are blue and white as they are always in high demand, along with violet and purple. This variety tends to bloom earlier than others; grows 24 to 36 inches (60 to 90 cm) tall.

Umbels

Ammi majus, **False Queen Anne's Lace;** *Ammi visnaga,* **Bishop's Weed;**
Anethum graveolens, **Dill;** *Daucus carota,* **Queen Anne's Lace, Wild Carrot**

Coming all from the same plant family and having a similar (umbel) shape, you may be wondering why I grow them all rather than picking a favorite. The reason is that their slight differences add variety to bouquets without causing a lot of extra fuss, since they all have similar growing requirements. We can stagger our use of them and, in that way, have wonderful fillers that are not the same every week.

These plants are well-loved by pollinators; it seems the smaller ones gravitate toward these blooms. They are also deer resistant, especially dill and *Daucus,* and all are great reseeders if some of the blooms are left to mature on the plant.

Transplant when leaves reach 3 to 5 inches tall. Top to bottom: False Queen Anne's Lace, Dill, Queen Anne's Lace

- **Seeding and growing tips:** Both *Ammi* and *Daucus* are started indoors in ¾-inch (2 cm) soil blocks. To get the very best germination rates, they prefer a temperature swing from mid-80s°F (mid-27°C) in the day to the upper 60s°F (upper 15.5°C) at night, so you might experiment with direct sowing them if your climate will provide these temperatures at some point leading into fall. We direct sow dill in the field in fall. All of these plants seem to benefit from row cover over winter.

- **Flower support notes:** Because of their tall, wiry stems and flower head shape that catches the wind, they benefit from flower support netting.

- **Harvesting and conditioning notes:** See Stage to harvest images (page 169). These plants produce a milky sap that can cause skin irritation, so I recommend wearing gloves and protective clothing when harvesting. Although beautiful at any stage, they

growing facts

Preferred season: Cool

Winter low temperature survival: 10°F (-12°C)

Starting from seed:

- Prefer to start seed indoors, except for dill (see following)
- Start seed indoors 4 to 6 weeks before planting outdoors
- Prefer to start in ¾-inch (2 cm) soil blocks
- Needs some light to sprout; cover only very lightly
- Soil temperature: 70°F (21°C; see growing tip following)
- 5 to 14 days to sprout
- Air temperature for optimal transplant growth: 60 to 70°F (15.5 to 21°C)
- Transplant to the garden when: 3 to 5 inches (7.5 to 13 cm) tall

Sun requirement: Full sun, at least 6 to 8 hours

Height: 24 to 48 inches (60 to 120 cm)

Rows of plants per 36-inch (90 cm)-wide bed: 3 to 4

Plant spacing in row: 6 inches (15 cm)

Days to bloom: 85 to 90

Flower support: Yes

Fertilization: Standard bed preparation (see page 57)

home garden tip

At the end of the season, leave a few flowers to mature and reseed the garden for next year.

Stage to harvest: Cut when the blooms are developing and a third of the tiny flowers are open up through developing seed heads yet pausing all harvesting during the shedding stages.

do go through a period of dropping pollen after flowering and before seed heads form. I try to avoid cutting them during that "in between" stage. Experiment with how early you can cut without drooping or wilting; I like to cut when just a few of the outside florets have opened. Make the first cut of the central stem almost at ground level, just above the lowest two or three side shoots. Future harvests can be made at the base of the stem. Follow the standard conditioning steps on page 32. *Ammi* and *Daucus* are sensitive to ethylene, whereas dill is not. They seem to benefit from the use of holding solution. With proper conditioning, expect fresh blooms to last 5 to 10 days in the vase. They can be dried at the seed head stage and are quite lovely that way.

- **Good to know:** Some varieties of this plant family may be considered invasive in some regions; check with your local agricultural authorities for more information.

Favorite Varieties

AMMI MAJUS

'Graceland' features large, flat, white flower clusters with an airy look that resembles the common wild-grown Queen Anne's lace; grows 36 to 48 inches (90 to 120 cm) tall.

AMMI VISNAGA

'Green Mist' has large, white, lacy blooms that are slightly more dome shaped than *Ammi majus* with a less airy look; grows 36 to 48 inches (90 to 120 cm) tall.

DAUCUS CAROTA

'Dara' has large, flat blooms that start out a deep mauve color, then gradually change to a soft green; grows 24 to 48 inches (60 to 120 cm) tall.

From left to right: 'Ammi majus' ready to harvest fresh and with some developing seed heads, 'Dill Bouquet', and Daucus 'Dara' with fresh blooms.

ANETHUM GRAVEOLENS

'Dill Bouquet' with tiny chartreuse yellow flowers in its umbel, this airy bloom looks like fireworks bursting throughout the garden, and it does the same in bouquets. This is the same variety commonly used as a culinary herb and pickling spice. The classic dill scent comes from the foliage, which can be stripped off completely, if desired; grows 24 to 60 inches (60 to 150 cm) tall.

flower farmer insider tip

Depending on your climate, you might be able to get successions planted after the very early spring planting. My fall plantings of *Ammi* and *Daucus* are very productive so successions beyond fall and very early spring plantings are not needed.

Xerochrysum bracteatum

Strawflower

We love this one as a dried flower, but it's also a fantastic long-lasting fresh flower with its lovely, bright colors. Native to Australia, strawflower likes a cool start but can tolerate a warm and dry summer as it matures. It features a center flower with papery bracts surrounding it; the bracts are what appear to be the petals of the strawflower. Strawflowers attract pollinators and are deer resistant.

- **Seeding and growing tips:** Strawflower seed does not store well, so for the best germination rates use the freshest seed possible—I buy new seed each year. Because they are surface-sown seeds, I use wide-weave burlap over soil blocks to keep them moist for the best germination, removing the burlap once 50 percent of the seeds have sprouted. Strawflower prefers well-drained soil and drier

Strawflower transplants just planted into the garden from ¾-inch blocks, 8 weeks before my last spring frost. Transplant when leaves are 3 to 5 inches long.

conditions, so does best in raised beds. Their best growth and flowering is typically while daytime temps are 70 to 75°F (21 to 24°C), but they can withstand warmer temperatures.

home garden tip

You may find shorter "bedding plant" varieties at your local nursery, which are great for containers and landscaping but not tall enough for cut flowers. To encourage continuous flowering, cut blooms as they mature. In my experience, strawflower is not a great reseeder.

growing facts

Preferred season: Cool

Winter low temperature survival: 10°F (-12°C)

Starting from seed:
- Prefer to start seed indoors
- Start seed indoors 4 to 6 weeks before planting outdoors
- Prefer to start in ¾-inch (2 cm) soil blocks
- Needs light to sprout; do not cover
- Soil temperature: 70 to 75°F (21 to 24°C)
- 7 to 10 days to sprout
- Air temperature for optimal transplant growth: 60 to 70°F (15.5 to 21°C)
- Transplant to the garden when: 3 to 5 inches (7.5 to 13 cm) tall

Sun requirement: Full sun

Height: 24 to 48 inches (60 to 120 cm)

Rows of plants per 36-inch (90 cm)-wide bed: 4

Plant spacing in row: 6 inches (15 cm)

Days to bloom: 75 to 85

Flower support: Yes

Fertilization: Standard bed preparation (see page 57); additional field applications may be beneficial

I pinch to encourage branching, which may result in an additional four to six stems per plant. See "Pinching Plants" (page 53). Plant 6 inches (15 cm) apart in the garden, allowing more space between plants for air circulation in wetter environments. Adding fertilizer by side dressing or drip irrigation may be beneficial in the field to continue vigorous blooming throughout the season.

- **Flower support notes:** I use flower support netting on all cutting garden plantings.

- **Harvesting and conditioning notes:** See Stage to harvest image (above). Harvest the central stem almost at ground level, just above the lowest three or four side shoots. Future harvests can be made at the base of the stem. For fresh and dried flowers, harvest when the first two or three layers of petals, called bracts, have unfolded but before the flower appears wide open. Avoid harvesting overmature wide-open blooms as they may shatter and discolor. I remove all the foliage below the top 6 inches (15 cm). Flowers with petals turned backward are too old and should be deadheaded. Because of its papery quality, this flower does not seem to benefit from floral preservatives nor is it ethylene sensitive. Expect fresh blooms to last 7 to 10 days in the vase.

- **Good to know:** Flowers can be dried on the stem, or just the blooms can be cut off and dried for use in crafts.

ABOVE, FROM LEFT *Stage to harvest: To prevent discoloring later in development, harvest when the first two to three rows of petals open and the center is just showing.*

A great view of the variation in bloom colors from upper left to right: King Size golden yellow, King Size silvery rose, Peach Mix, and King Size white, orange, and raspberry.

Favorite Varieties

'Cut Flower' series produces large 2- to 3-inch (5 to 7.5 cm) flowers on sturdy stems. They bloom in a wide range of colors, such as orange, white, rose, silvery rose, golden yellow, fireball, and lemon yellow; grows 30 to 48 inches (75 to 120 cm) tall.

'King Size' mix includes 2-inch (5 cm,) blooms in yellow, white, orange, and pink; grows 20 to 30 inches (50 to 75 cm) tall.

'Monstrosum' series is a popular variety among flower farmers, offering tall, strong stems and large 2- to 3-inch (5 to 7.5 cm) double blooms. This series includes gold, magenta, orange, and rose colors; grows to 36 inches (90 cm) tall.

flower farmer insider tip

Strawflowers are an important ingredient in our mixed bouquets. There is strong demand for this flower from florists and for supermarket bunches. I like to grow all the colors but lean heavialy on white, rose, gold, and peach varieties. My first planting is 6 to 8 weeks before the last spring frost, followed by succession plantings every 4 weeks for at least two additional plantings. There are several unnamed seed varieties in gorgeous colors for sale, and, as long as they list a tall enough stem length, I try them. Any fresh crop not sold is always dried.

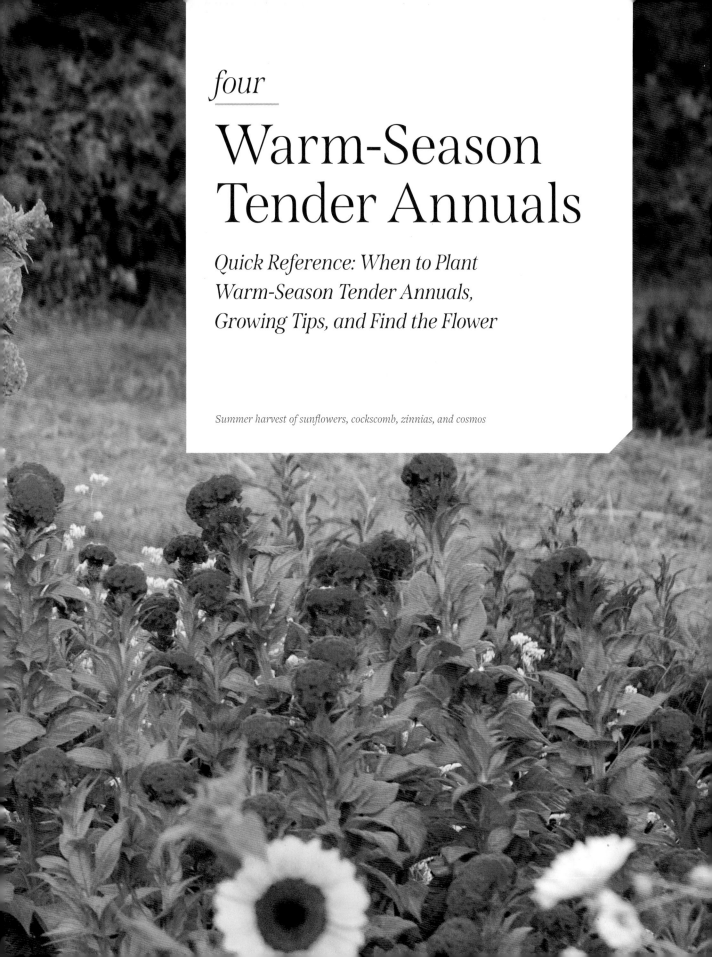

four

Warm-Season Tender Annuals

Quick Reference: When to Plant Warm-Season Tender Annuals, Growing Tips, and Find the Flower

Summer harvest of sunflowers, cockscomb, zinnias, and cosmos

PLANT WARM-SEASON TENDER ANNUALS in the garden as conditions begin to warm with summer just around the corner or in full swing.

Transplant once the soil temperature has reached 60°F (15.5°C), or plant seeds in the garden when soil temperatures have reached 65°F (18°C). These plants thrive in warm to hot conditions.

Find the Flower

PAGE NUMBER	COMMON NAME	BOTANICAL NAME
178	Amaranth	*Amaranthus caudatus, Amaranthus cruentus*
210	Basil	*Ocimum basilicum, Ocimum basilicum var. citriodora*
181	Celosia: cockscomb	*Celosia cristata*
182	Celosia: feather	*Celosia plumosa*
183	Celosia: wheat	*Celosia spicata*
188	Cosmos	*Cosmos bipinnatus*
193	Eucalyptus	*Eucalyptus*
196	Globe amaranth	*Gomphrena globosa, Gomphrena haagean*
213	Gourd vine	*Cucurbita Pepo var. Ovifera*
200	Grass: 'Frosted Explosion'	*Panicum elegans*
201	Grass: 'Green Drops'	*Panicum violaceum*
201	Grass: 'Purple Majesty Millet'	*Pennisetum glaucum*
201	Grass: 'Lime Light Millet,' 'Hylander,' 'Lowlander'	*Setaria italica*
207	Hibiscus	*Hibiscus acetosella*
217	Hyacinth bean vine	*Dolichos lablab*
218	Hairy balls	*Gomphocarpus physocarpus*
215	Love-in-a-puff vine	*Cardiospermum halicacabum*
221	Marigold	*Tagetes erecta*
220	Pumpkin-on-a-stick	*Solanum integrifolium*
202	Sunflower	*Helianthus annus*
220	Striped garden egg	*Solanum aethiopicum var. gilo*
224	Zinnia	*Zinnia elegans*

COCKSCOMB PUMPKIN-ON-A-STICK

COSMOS

FEATHER CELOSIA

SUNFLOWERS

GRASSES

Amaranthus caudatus, Amaranthus cruentus

Amaranth

Amaranth produces blooms in rich, warm colors, making them perfect for late-summer and fall bouquets. An added bonus is they also grow and bloom faster under the short days of fall. The colors range from chartreuse green to burgundy red to amber copper and even some spectacular bicolor combinations.

The bloom shapes are as varied as the colors. Just when I think 'Dreadlocks' is my favorite, with its funky, drooping lumpy ball blooms, 'Autumn Touch' starts putting out thick green upright plumes that turn copper, and I quickly change my mind and absolutely fall in love with them. No wonder some think amaranth blooms are straight out of a Dr. Seuss storybook, with amazing shapes and colors that make useful cut flowers.

Transplant to the garden when 3 to 5 inches tall. To prevent tangled seedling stems, as on left, monitor the sprouting stage closely and move to the grow light as soon as they begin sprouting.

growing facts

Preferred season: Warm

Starting from seed:
- Prefer to start seed indoors; can also be sown in the garden
- Start seed indoors 3 to 4 weeks before planting outdoors
- Prefer to start in ¾-inch (2 cm) soil blocks
- Needs light to sprout; firmly seat the seed on the soil's surface to make good contact, covering lightly
- Soil temperature: 70 to 80°F (21 to 27°C)
- 1 to 8 days to sprout
- Air temperature for optimal transplant growth: 75 to 90°F (24 to 32°C)
- Transplant to the garden when: 4 to 6 inches (10 to 15 cm) tall

Sun requirement: Minimum 8 hours, more is better

Height: 36 to 72 inches (90 to 180 cm)

Rows of plants per 36-inch (90 cm)-wide bed: 4

Plant spacing in row: 6 inches (15 cm)

Days to bloom: 65 to 75

Flower support: Yes

Fertilization: Standard bed preparation (see page 57)

- **Seeding and growing tips:** Amaranth seedlings can quickly become tall and tangled, which makes them difficult to care for and even harder to plant. To prevent this problem, pay close attention to germination, which can happen in less than 24 hours for some, and move the trays under the grow light as soon as a few seeds start cracking. Beyond standard bed preparation, I do not fertilize in the field. Amaranth thrives in nutrient-poor soil. Overly rich conditions can produce soft, weak stems. Tight plant spacing and pinching the plants produce the most usable stems and blooms. Flowers can grow so large it limits their uses, so don't be afraid to crowd the plants in the bed.

- **Flower support notes:** Installing support netting is beneficial to support the heavy, giant blooms.

- **Harvesting and conditioning notes:** See Stage to harvest image (above). Make the

Stage to harvest: As soon as a third of the tiny flowers are open. 1. 'Hot Biscuits' 2. 'Dreadlocks' 3. 'Towers Green' 4. 'Autumn's Touch' 5. 'Oeschberg' 6. 'Velvet Curtains' 7. 'Mira' 8. 'Coral Fountains.'

cut at the base of the stem (see illustration: Where to Make the Cut on Branching Annuals, page 30). Follow the standard conditioning steps on page 57. Harvest amaranth with half to three-fourths of the tiny flowers developed on the head. When harvested too late, yellow pollen will begin to appear at the tip of the flower and will drop onto tabletops. I strip any foliage that shows pest damage. Flowers last 7 to 14 days in the vase.

home garden tip

For a fun display in the garden, skip pinching a few of the plants so they produce novel whopper blooms.

flower farmer insider tip

Growers who experience heavy pest pressure growing amaranth must weigh whether this flower is worth the potential associated costs and losses. I found it impossible to grow dahlias and amaranth in the same season because the pests attracted to the amaranth caused major dahlia bloom damage. Sometimes, pest control is simply eliminating the crop that attracts the pests.

Amaranth does not require or benefit from cooler storage.

- **Good to know:** Amaranth blooms dry easily by hanging them in a dry warm place. Harvest flowers after florets are fully open and the flower feels firm to the touch. Hang erect plume types upside-down and stand the drooping-type blooms upright in a container to allow them to dry in their natural form.

Amaranth is a super fun flower to grow because of its potential whopper and quirky blooms. A great fall flower!

Favorite Varieties

Pinch All
(see "Pinching Plants," page 53)

AMARANTHUS CAUDATUS

Draping blooms: all grow 36 to 60 inches (90 to 150 cm) tall

'Coral Fountain' has a coral color that makes this flower a good one to grow throughout the season.

'Dreadlocks' is a red bloom with large bumps on the flower.

'Mira' I love this one! Blooms have a mix of green, rose, and red on a hanging bloom; fun to use in bouquets.

AMARANTHUS CRUENTUS

Upright blooms: all grow 40 to 72 inches (100 to 180 cm) tall

'Autumn's Touch' emerges green and develops brushes of copper on the bloom with age.

'Green Towers' is a chartreuse green bloom useful in any bouquet.

'Hot Biscuits' has plumes that age to a deep honey color and that works well as a filler flower in bouquets.

'Oeschberg' is a fall favorite for bouquets, with a deep wine color and cute wispy spiked flowers.

'Velvet Curtains' is a thick wine-colored bloom with a red stem and foliage.

Celosia cristata, Celosia plumosa, Celosia spicata

Cockscomb, Feather Celosia, Wheat Celosia

The bright-colored, long-lasting, and sometimes unusual-looking blooms in the *Celosia* family have made them one of the most popular and in-demand groups of flowers that I grow. They thrive in warm to hot growing conditions, with their peak performance during the long, hot days of summer.

Celosia includes three different types of blooms I find easy to grow: *C. cristata*, commonly called cockscomb, with big blooms full of funky ribs and crevasses; *C. plumosa* known as feather celosia, with fluffy plumes; and *C. spicata*, called wheat celosia, with a trimmer, finer plume. Within each type of bloom, there are many varieties. My favorites include a rich, diverse harvest of colors, textures, and shapes.

Celosia can be tricky to know which stage of blooming is best to harvest for cut flowers. As I became familiar with their seed development stages, it became easier to recognize when I

should cut the flowers. Learning the proper harvesting stages for this flower opened a door to a lot of terrific cut flowers. I have had few issues with pests and diseases within this plant family. Prolonged rainy weather can cause problems in beds that don't have good drainage, and mature blooms can rot in ongoing wet conditions.

Cockscomb

Celosia cristata landed its common name, cockscomb, because the bloom is very similar to the comb on a rooster's head. There are two different types of bloom shapes among the cockscomb

ABOVE *Stage to harvest: The cockscomb on the right is ready to harvest before seed development. The one on the left is old and dirty with seeds developing.*

growing facts

Preferred season: Warm

Starting from seed:
- Prefer to start seed indoors
- Start seed indoors 4 to 6 weeks before planting outdoors
- Prefer to start in ¾-inch (2 cm) soil blocks
- Needs light to sprout; firmly seat the seed on the soil's surface to make good contact
- Soil temperature: 75 to 85°F (24 to 29°C)
- 7 to 14 days to sprout
- Air temperature for optimal transplant growth: 75 to 90°F (24 to 32°C)
- Transplant to the garden when: 3 to 5 inches (7.5 to 13 cm) tall

Sun requirement: Minimum 8 hours, more is better

Height: 28 to 60 inches (70 to 150 cm)

Rows of plants per 36-inch (90 cm)-wide bed: 4 to 8

Plant spacing in row: 6 inches (15 cm)

Days to bloom: 70 to 120 days

Flower support: Yes

Fertilization: Standard bed preparation (see page 57)

varieties: the fan and the ball. The fan blooms are flat on the sides with the combs and ribs on the top and the sides where the seed develops. The ball bloom has more combs and ribs that tumble over the sides of the bloom and cover the developing seed area and grow into the shape of a ball. A characteristic of some of the fan-type varieties is that they are slower to develop seeds. That keeps the sides of the blooms looking cleaner—a big deal for a cut flower. There are branching and single-stem cockscomb varieties, and the plant spacing is different for each. Branching varieties are four rows in a 36-inch (90 cm)-wide bed; single-stem varieties are eight rows in a 36-inch (90 cm)-wide bed; both are planted 6 inches (15 cm) apart in the row. Single-stem varieties do not get pinched.

home garden tip

Celosia is a strong self-seeder when blooms are left in the garden to develop and scatter seeds that will sprout into new plants.

Feather Celosia

Celosia plumosa became known as feather celosia because the blooms are fuzzy and resemble feathers. This group of blooms came to play a significant role in my cutting garden with their uniform growth and abundant production of

long, straight stems with large colorful blooms. I grow several varieties in a full spectrum of colors. Pinching the plants in this group has proven very beneficial and can double the stem production of the non-pinched plant. With all the new varieties and color selections available in recent years, selecting which to grow can be difficult. I recommend growing the mixed colors of any given variety when it is new to you to have firsthand experience with what may be your most useful or favorite color.

Wheat Celosia

Celosia spicata is a smaller group of plants called wheat celosia because its upright slender blooms look like sheaves of wheat. A sheaf is how wheat stems are bound together with all their heads gathered tightly. The blooms in this group may not seem as showy or as big as their cousins in the feather celosia group, but I find they contribute in other ways. Their foliage can be more interesting, and some varieties change colors as the plant ages. 'Hi-Z' is one of my all-time favorites with its reddish stem,

Celosia plumes are in my top ten production crops. From the left: 'Cramer's Amazon', 'Sylphid', 'Sunday' orange, 'Hi-Z', and 'Flamingo Feather'.

chartreuse green foliage with red veining, and a magenta bloom. All in this group produce a vast number of uniform long stems.

- **Seeding and growing tips:** Starting *Celosia* seeds indoors and growing the transplants under grow lights for the recommended 16 hours of light a day helps prevent the transplants from setting blooms prematurely. Although these plants are drought tolerant once established and aren't fussy about fertilization, they produce best with regular waterings and feedings for the longest stems and biggest flowers. The short day lengths and cooler temperatures of spring and fall can induce blooming on shorter stems along with slowing vegetative growth and bloom development. Shorter days can also speed seed development, so flowers may need to be harvested more frequently.

- **Flower support notes:** I use support netting on all *Celosia* plantings. I recommend closer placement of support-netting stakes for cockscomb plantings as their stems are often towering at 48 inches (120 cm) tall and the large, heavy heads create a canopy of flowers that can go down easily in a rainstorm.

- **Harvesting and conditioning notes:** See Stage to harvest image (page 181). Make the cut at the base of the stem (see illustration: Where to Make the Cut on Branching Annuals (page 30). Follow the standard conditioning steps on page 32. Harvesting with the largest bloom before they begin to develop seeds can be a challenge. When harvested too late, the flowers appear old and dirty as the black seeds have begun to develop and will go on to scatter seeds from the vase as the process continues. Recognizing the stage to harvest gets easier with practice. *Celosias* do not require or benefit from cooler storage. Expect the flowers to last 10 to 14 days in the vase.

Favorite Varieties

Cockscomb Branching: Pinch (see "Pinching Plants," page 53)

CELOSIA CRISTATA

'**Asuka**' has textured ribs that give the fan blooms a different look from other cockscombs,

in colors of green, red, orange, pink, and purple; grows 36 inches (90 cm) tall.

'Chief' is my go-to cockscomb variety for its ball shape and heavy branching, in colors of rose, scarlet, red-orange, gold, and persimmon; grows 36 to 48 inches (90 to 120 cm) tall.

'Cramer' was specially bred for its drying qualities and its fan-type bloom that also makes a great fresh cut, in colors of green, rose, and burgundy; grows 36 to 48 inches (90 to 120 cm) tall.

'Supercrest' includes some gigantic and funky mostly fan blooms in colors of green, orange, pink, red, and yellow; grows 48 to 60 inches (120 to 150 cm) tall.

flower farmer insider tip with
Dr. Emily Nekl, Fuggles Flowers

HARVESTING *CELOSIA* SEEDS

- Tag your favorite flowers by color or shape.
- To isolate special characteristics through self-pollination, bag flower heads in organza bags before they start opening.
- Harvest heads when ½ inch (1 cm) of color remains at the tips. Expect to lose seed during harvest.
- Harvest in the afternoon after 3 days of dry weather.
- Cut at the base of the heads.
- Dry on a porous material, like newspaper, and turn heads daily, allowing them to dry out. The process takes 7 to 10 days.
- Shake the heads and mature seeds will release.
- Screen with fine-mesh wire to remove the chaff.
- Store in a cool dry place until seed-starting time.

FROM LEFT *Stage to harvest: Plumes on the left are fresh and clean ready for harvest. The plumes on the right are old and appear dirty because they are developing seeds.*

Transplant to the garden when 3 to 5 inches tall.

185

flower farmer insider tip

One of the benefits of growing the single-stem varieties is that they can be succession planted weekly for a consistent supply. The branching varieties that produce several stems over a period of time follow our succession recipe of planting every few weeks. These long-lasting flowers played a major role in our mixed bouquet supermarket business.

Cockscomb Single Stem: Do Not Pinch

'Act' has a rich family of colors on fan blooms, including chartreuse green, purple, yellow, and red; grows 50 inches (125 cm) tall.

'Coral Unlimited' has gorgeous big fans in shades of salmon and coral with amazing stems; grows 36 to 48 inches (90 to 120 cm) tall.

'Spring Green' is my favorite green fan bloom, a great filler flower. I start weekly succession planting all summer; grows 36 to 48 inches (90 to 120 cm) tall.

Plumes Branching: Pinch (see "Pinching Plants," page 53)

CELOSIA PLUMOSA

'Sunday Series' is available in a mix or individual colors, including orange, bright pink, cherry, purple, pink, gold, yellow, white, and green; grows 28 to 40 inches (70 to 100 cm) tall.

'Sylphid' is a greenish-white plume that has proven to be one of the most versatile and useful plumes I grow; grows 36 to 48 inches (90 to 120 cm) tall.

'Texas Plumes' is a dynamite mix of bright and soft colors with large fluffy blooms, in colors of soft yellow, shrimp, green-white, gold, pink, magenta, orange; grows 36 to 48 inches (90 to 120 cm) tall.

Plumes Branching: Pinch
(see "Pinching Plants," page 53)

CELOSIA SPICATA
'Celway' plumes have multiple spikes on each bloom and add great interest to bouquets, in colors of orange, purple, red, salmon, terracotta, and white; grows 40 to 48 inches (100 to 120 cm) tall.

'Flamingo Feather' has the softest blush color that is useful and dries beautifully; grows 30 to 48 inches (75 to 120 cm) tall.

'Hi-Z' has been a longtime favorite with its magenta bloom and red-green stems and foliage; grows 36 to 48 inches (90 to 120 cm) tall.

BELOW *Lisa and Emily Nekl in the first field of custom grown Celosia Texas Plume seeds for The Gardener's Workshop. Emily is now using isolation tents and growing even more specialty seeds for us.*

FAR LEFT *My go-to favorite branching cockscomb is 'Chief' for the fantastic colors and its high production. From the top: rose, gold, persimmon, scarlet, corona, and red-orange.*

Cosmos bipinnatus

Cosmos

Nothing else is quite like cosmos, with their cheerful faces and wispy foliage. As beautiful as they are, we didn't grow cosmos during our fast-paced high-production farming years. Now that we're slowing down and growing more variety, we've really enjoyed having cosmos back in the mix again. Cosmos have some quirks as cut flowers, but they are generally easy to grow and very prolific. There are some newer varieties that really extend their color palette, and we're having fun growing them all.

Cosmos are a short day–length flower. The secret to great longer-lasting cosmos is to have plants in the ground coming along and/or ready to bloom in mid to late summer and into fall as the day lengths begin to shorten. It took me a

couple of years of making these flowers a bigger part of my cutting garden to crack this code. Oh, how easy it is to overlook major details like this when there are so many flowers to grow! Bringing in heavier plantings in my last two warm-season succession plantings brought so much more abundance, better quality flowers, and they hydrated more easily. I still plant some earlier in the season to accent bouquets, but it's these later plantings that produce abundant cosmos bouquets that take your breath away!

My reintroduction to cosmos aligned with many new variety introductions in spectacular colors. The focus when planning succession plantings is to include the colors best suited for the season in which that planting will be blooming. I am so smitten with most of the varieties that I plant a little of each in all the successions, with an emphasis on whites and pinks in the next-to-last succession, then the last planting is heavy on 'Rubenza', 'Apricotta', 'Xsenia', and 'Double Click' cranberry. Fall bouquets will never be the same without these gems.

I rank cosmos as a cut flower in the same category as sweet peas that have a similar shorter vase life. Their time in a vase may be shorter than most other cut flowers I grow, but so worth growing. I've learned that a big vase of light and airy cosmos blossoms on the kitchen counter for a short but glorious time is more memorable than other flowers I grow. My Members-Only Flower Market customers agreed—they were a sellout every week we had them. We all love cosmos.

- **Seeding and growing tips:** Plant cosmos in ¾-inch (2 cm) soil blocks leaving the "tail" of the seed to protrude from the top of the block, if necessary. This gives the seed the cover and darkness it needs to germinate. Cosmos are fast-growing seedlings, so when about half have sprouted, move the tray from the seedling heat mat to the grow light and provide 16 hours of light per day. I do not fertilize

home garden tip

Because cosmos are also a favorite of pollinators, plant some in your landscape for them to enjoy. Butterflies are especially fond of the large, open blooms, so try to resist cutting at this late stage as they don't make very good cut flowers anyway. Keep these pollinator plantings blooming by cutting off old blooms, also known as "deadheading."

ABOVE, FROM TOP *Transplant to the garden when 3 to 5 inches tall. Grown in the Swift Block Mini 75.*

Stage to harvest: Cut stems as the buds start to crack open to prevent bug damage and for the best vase life.

OPPOSITE *'Fizzy White' is one of the most productive and long-lasting cosmos I grow. I love the extra petals that make it frilly.*

seedlings in the tray. Being native to Mexico, they prefer drier soil and humid weather. Beyond my standard bed preparation, I do not fertilize in the field. Cosmos thrive in nutrient-poor soil. Too much fertility tends to make them grow lots of foliage and hardly any flowers. Too much water can also cause the plants to grow mostly foliage.

- **Flower support notes:** Support is crucial for cosmos—installing support netting is beneficial to support the many branches of these plants.

- **Harvesting and conditioning notes:** See Stage to harvest image (page 189). Harvest just as the bloom is cracking open to a few petals laying open. Make the cut at the base of the stem (see illustration: Where to Make the Cut on Branching Annuals, page 30). For the best hydration, strip off most of the foliage. Follow the standard conditioning steps on page 32. When harvested at the appropriate stage, expect flowers to last 5 to 7 days in the vase.

- **Good to know:** In warmer climates, garden cosmos can be a heavy reseeder and may become naturalized as a "weed" of sorts. However, the hybrid varieties mentioned following that we grow typically do not have this issue.

growing facts

Preferred season: Warm

Starting from seed:
- Prefer to start seed indoors; can also be sown in the garden
- Start seed indoors 4 to 6 weeks before planting outdoors
- Prefer to start in ¾-inch (2 cm) soil blocks
- Needs darkness to sprout (see seeding and growing tips following)
- Soil temperature: 75°F (24°C)
- 5 to 10 days to sprout
- Air temperature for optimal transplant growth: 75 to 90°F (24 to 32°C)
- Transplant to the garden when: 3 to 5 inches (7.5 to 13 cm) tall

Sun requirement: Minimum 8 hours, more is better

Height: 36 to 48 inches (90 to 120 cm)

Rows of plants per 36-inch (90 cm)-wide bed: 4

Plant spacing in row: 6 inches (15 cm)

Days to bloom: 85 to 100

Flower support: Yes

Fertilization: Standard bed preparation (see page 57)

Favorite Varieties

Pinch Unless Otherwise Noted (see "Pinching Plants," page 53)

'Afternoon White' is the largest and showiest white flower I have grown. Its bright-white blooms pop with its golden-yellow center, and it has sturdy stems. This is the cosmos that rekindled my love for these flowers. With white flowers fitting into every season, this one offers versatility, making it a complement of many color combinations and styles. It is especially spectacular as a bouquet by itself! With 2- to 4-inch (5 to10 cm) blooms, this one grows 36 to 48 inches (90 to 120 cm) tall.

'**Apricot Lemonade**' has a small bloom compared to other cosmos, but the bicolor coloring on these blooms creates a dreamy range of buttery lemon, apricot, and pink with the undersides of the blooms aging to soft yellow and rose-pink hues. In my garden, this flower was a fun, whimsical addition, but I found it difficult to harvest at the right stage for use in bouquets in general; grows 20 to 30 inches (50 to 75 cm) tall with 2-inch (5 cm) blooms.

'**Apricotta**' is one of the cosmos I especially love all by itself in a bouquet. The variety of soft apricot to pink blooms makes it a great wedding flower, yet it also works in fall. It is one of the most productive varieties. Some blooms will also have another row of smaller blade-like petals in the center; grows 36 to 48 inches (90 to 120 cm) tall with 3-inch (7.5 cm) blooms.

'**Cupcake**' is named for its scallop-edged petals that resemble cupcake wrappers. In my garden, this series is beautiful but does not produce as much abundance as others. It's this unique bloom's frilly smaller center petals that keep me growing them. Available in white and blush; grows to 36 inches (90 cm) tall.

'**Double Click**' is a beautiful mix of double and semidouble frilly blooms in an array of colors. I find this series performs best later in the season, giving a longer vase life and fewer drooping heads from the heavy blooms. The cranberry color in this series is especially perfect for fall bouquets. Other colors include pink bicolor, snow puff, rose, and violet bicolor; grows 36 to 48 inches (90 to 120 cm) tall with 2- to 3-inch (5 to 7.5 cm) blooms.

'**Fizzy White**' has been a top performer in my garden and seems to have an extended vase life.

Its large, tufted white blooms make it useful throughout the growing season in mixed and stand-alone bouquets; grows 36 to 60 inches (90 to 150 cm) tall with 2½- to 4-inch (6 to 10 cm) blooms.

'**Rubenza**' is the most perfect color for fall! This variety offers large blooms in shades of ruby-red cranberry. My favorite feature is that the

BELOW, CLOCKWISE FROM LEFT *Colors and blooms for every need. 1. 'Double Click' white 2. 'Double Click' Rose Bonbon 3. 'Double Click' cranberries 4. 'Afternoon White' 5. 'Apricotta' 6. 'Sensation' 7. 'Double Click' violet bicolor.*

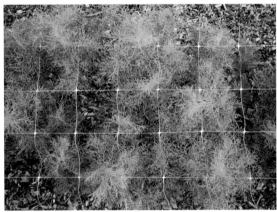

flower farmer insider tip

Harvesting cosmos can be time-consuming but must be done regularly because they open so quickly. I harvest daily when possible to get the most pest damage–free blooms, the best vase life, and keep the plant blooming. For ongoing, abundant, and high quality cosmos harvests, plant every 3 to 4 weeks to keep a bumper crop of blooms waiting in the garden.

petals fade as they age to a softer, lighter hue, just like a favorite pair of blue jeans. It is one of the few flowers that gets better with age; grows 36 to 48 inches (90 to 120 cm) tall with 2½- to 3½-inch (6 to 8.5 cm) blooms.

'Sensation' has large, single flowers with yellow centers in a mixture of pink, purple, cranberry, white, and bicolors. If I could only grow one cosmos, it would be 'Sensation', with the greatest mix of colors. This heirloom variety, tested by horticultural professionals, was deemed a top garden performer and won the All-American Award in 1936; grows 30 to 48 inches (75 to 120 cm) tall with 3- to 4-inch (7.5 to 10 cm) blooms.

'Xanthos' has a smaller, soft buttercream yellow bloom that grows on a more compact plant. I found this variety to grow tall enough to make it a worthy cut flower. Some blooms will also have another row of smaller blade-like petals in the center. I do not pinch this variety, as the resulting stems may be shorter than needed for bouquets; grows 20 to 25 inches (50 to 63 cm) tall with 2½-inch (6 cm) blooms.

'Xsenia' is a single-bloom cosmos with vibrant, glowing shades of raspberry on a compact plant. Petals age to a soft antique rose color, making it a great choice for fall bouquets. I do not pinch this variety, as the resulting stems may be shorter than needed for bouquets; grows 20 to 25 inches (50 to 63 cm) tall with 2½-inch (6 cm) blooms.

Eucalyptus
Eucalyptus

Eucalyptus is a fragrant, sturdy foliage plant that is fabulous in bouquets and arrangements. Grown as a large shrub, and even trees in mild winter regions, I grow it as an annual in my garden, where the average winter low temperature is 15°F (-9°C). The main challenge with eucalyptus is that it is painstakingly slow growing. Compared to the other annual plants I grow, it is slow to sprout, slow to grow into a transplantable size, and slow growing in the garden. In the garden, to give the plants the longest possible time to grow the longest and most abundant stems, have mature, robust transplants ready to transplant into the garden as soon as temperatures allow in spring.

home garden tip

Experiment with growing eucalyptus in large containers that can be brought inside over winter. One happy second- or third-year plant in a large pot will produce many stems.

Stage to harvest: Allow the stem tips to fully develop to prevent tip wilting. Eucalyptus is a favorite foliage for fresh and dried use. It is available in several varieties with varying leaf shapes and sizes. Left to right: 'Parvula Gum', 'Silver Drop', 'Silver Dollar', and 'Polyanthemos'.

flower farmer insider tip

The "seeded" eucalyptus that florists often use is actually eucalyptus in its budding stage, which happens during the second season of growth. If your climate is too cold to keep eucalyptus alive over winter, you will not be able to get a plant to the budding stage. In that case, you will need either to provide appropriate heated cover for it to grow year-round or grow it as an annual for the foliage only and cut all stems before the first frost in fall. See my wintering over strategy following.

BELOW, FROM LEFT Each year, I attempt to winter over my plants because the best harvests are from 2- and 3-year-old plants. I have just enough occasional success to keep me doing it each season. I prune the plants to 12 inches (30 cm) tall at the end of the season, mulch with leaves 12 inches (30 cm) deep, and hoop and cover with two layers of row cover.

Transplant to the garden when 3 to 5 inches tall. Pictured transplants are 12-weeks old. They started in the ¾-inch soil block and moved up to the 2-inch soil block at 3 weeks old.

Known to many as "gum trees," there are more than seven hundred species of eucalyptus in the wild, but only a handful of varieties are commonly used in the cut-flower industry. Eucalyptus is native to Australia, where the majority of the international seed crop is currently produced. Recent forest fires in Australia have caused some varieties to be in very short supply temporarily, but the silver lining has been that more varieties of seeds have recently come to market, offering gardeners and farmers a broader selection of varieties, textures, leaf sizes, and subtle differences in color.

Eucalyptus may take a little more care and time to grow useable stems, but, as a gardener and a farmer, I find it very worth the extra effort. With each passing season, it has become easier to grow.

- **Seeding and growing tips:** Eucalyptus is always one of the first seeds we start in late winter because it takes 10 to 12 weeks to get a good size transplant. I start seeds in ¾-inch (2 cm) soil blocks, and this is one of the few that I move up to the 2-inch (5 cm) block size to continue growing into the most mature

growing facts

Preferred season: Warm

Starting from seed:

- Prefer to start seed indoors
- Start seed indoors 10 to 12 weeks before planting outdoors
- Prefer to start in ¾-inch (2 cm) soil blocks
- Needs light to sprout
- Soil temperature: 70°F (21°C)
- 14 to 21 days to sprout
- Air temperature for optimal transplant growth: 75 to 90°F (24 to 32°C)
- Transplant to the garden when: 3 to 5 inches (7.5 to 13 cm) tall

Sun requirement: Minimum 8 hours, more is better

Height: 24 to 36 inches (60 to 90 cm)

Rows of plants per 36-inch (90 cm)-wide bed: 2

Plant spacing in row: 6 inches (15 cm)

Days to bloom: Foliage only

Flower support: No

Fertilization: Standard bed preparation (see page 57)

robust transplants possible. Pinching is beneficial to get branching earlier; however it will increase the growing time needed to reach a longer stem length.

- **Flower support notes:** Not recommended

- **Harvesting and conditioning notes:** See Stage to harvest image (page 193). Stems may be harvested at any time after leaves start to feel leathery and hardened. Make the cut at the base of the stem (see illustration: Where to Make the Cut on Branching Annuals, page 30). Sap can seep from cut stems and after lower leaf removal, so it is recommended to wear gloves to harvest. Follow the standard conditioning steps on page 32. Expect stems to last 1 to 3 weeks in the vase. Once initially hydrated, eucalyptus can be used out of water for events or photo shoots. Eucalyptus can be stored in a cooler at 35 to 38°F (2 to 3°C).

- **Good to know:** Eucalyptus can also be dried by bunching and hanging upside-down, or it can be preserved with vegetable glycerin.

Favorite Varieties

Pinch All
(see "Pinching Plants," page 53)

'Parvula Gum' has a look different from the typical eucalyptus, with its small blue-green leaves; grows 24 inches (60 cm) tall.

'Polyanthemos' has rounded blue-green leaves with flexible stems, allowing them to shimmer in the breeze like dangling earrings; grows 24 inches (60 cm) tall.

'Silver Dollar' has large silvery-gray leaves and has long been a favorite among florists; grows 24 to 36 inches (60 to 90 cm) tall.

'Silver Drop' is similar to 'Silver Dollar' in shape, but is smaller in leaf size and has beautiful coloring; grows 24 to 36 inches (60 to 90 cm) tall.

Gomphrena globosa, Gomphrena haageana

Globe Amaranth

Better known as globe amaranth, *Gomphrena* is a small but powerful flower. The globe-shaped blooms are a welcome addition to bouquets, providing a nice contrast to flatter-faced flowers such as sunflowers and zinnias. Our commercial customers and the bouquet makers on my farm always loved having plenty of *Gomphrena* to embellish bouquets because there really isn't another flower that brings a bouncy little ball into a bouquet.

home garden tip

The crafting options with this dried flower are endless. They're great in wreaths, wearables like rings, bracelets, and hairpieces, even in potpourri or bath salts.

We affectionately call it "Gomphie," but it wasn't always that way. As much as everyone else loved it, it was one of the flowers I chose not to grow during our high-production years. For one, it produced smaller flowers on shorter stems that seem to take forever to fill a harvest bucket when compared to other summer annuals—a real downer when faced with harvesting thousands of other flowers. Plus, the plant's heavily branching nature can make it even more challenging to harvest because plants can have tangled stems and some are brittle and break easily.

Fortunately, as a result of the cut-flower industry growing so much in recent years, new plant introductions are coming out. 'Audray', a recent introduction, is the variety that rekindled my love of Gomphie. Trialing her white color selection revealed the improved growth habit and tougher stems. Bringing this plant

FROM LEFT *Gomphrena benefits from flower support netting as the stems should be harvested when fully developed and the canopy gets top heavy.*

Transplant when they reach 3 to 5 inches tall. Grown in the ¾-inch soil block and ready to go to the garden.

back into our succession planting also aligned with my exploration of drying flowers. I began drying all leftover flowers just to see how they performed, and *Gomphrena*, known as an everlasting, was a shining star that air-dries easily, retaining its brilliant color.

- **Seeding and growing tips:** To provide the darkness *Gomphrena* needs to germinate, push the seed into the block about ⅛ inch (0.3 cm) deep. As a Central American native, *Gomphrena* thrives in hot conditions. Pinching is not necessary as this plant branches heavily naturally. Close 6-inch (15 cm) spacing in all directions typically grows taller straighter stems.

- **Flower support notes:** Not recommended due to its thick stems and shorter, branching growing habit.

- **Harvesting and conditioning notes:** See stage of harvest photo (page 198). Harvest

growing facts

Preferred season: Warm

Starting from seed:
- Prefer to start seed indoors
- Start seed indoors 4 to 5 weeks before planting outdoors
- Prefer to start in ¾-inch (2 cm) soil blocks
- Needs darkness to sprout; cover lightly with soil
- Soil temperature: 70°F (21°C)
- 7 to 12 days to sprout
- Air temperature for optimal transplant growth: 75 to 90°F (24 to 32°C)
- Transplant to the garden when: 3 to 5 inches (7.5 to 13 cm) tall

Sun requirement: Minimum 8 hours, more is better

Height: 24 to 30 inches (60 to 75 cm)

Rows of plants per 36-inch (90 cm)-wide bed: 6

Plant spacing in row: 6 inches (15 cm)

Days to bloom: 85 to 100

Flower support: Yes

Fertilization: Standard bed preparation (see page 57)

Stage to harvest: Allow the flowers to fully develop before cutting. Gomphrena is an excellent flower for flower crowns, crafts, and boutonnieres because it holds up out of water. Tucker sporting a crown that will also dry beautifully.

when blooms are fully developed, when large and round but not elongated and developing seed yet. I make the cut at ground level, below the junction of several stems, almost cutting the entire plant. Strip the foliage on the lower half of the stems. If you harvest before the blooms are fully developed, you'll have some with droopy stems that cannot be revived. Once cut, remove the small side shoots, leaving only the fully formed blooms. If using fresh, follow the standard conditioning steps on page 32. Expect fresh blooms to last 10 to 20 days in the vase. Alternatively, hang in bunches to dry or cut off individual blooms to use in crafts. *Gomphrena* does not require or benefit from cooler storage.

- **Good to know:** As a member of the Amaranth plant family, *Gomphrena* is edible and so is safe to use as a decoration on food, such as cakes.

Favorite Varieties

Do Not Pinch

GOMPHRENA GLOBOSA

'Audray' has the best growth habit for harvesting. The white in the series doesn't get prematurely dirty looking, which is a great benefit, especially if drying. Other colors include purple, bicolor rose, and red-purple; grows 36 inches (90 cm) tall with 1-inch (2.5 cm) blooms.

'Tall' includes vibrant colors that resemble dangling jewels in our bouquets. The purple color is fantastic! Available as a mix and individual colors such as deep pink and purple; grows 28 inches (70 cm) tall with 1-inch (2.5 cm) blooms.

GOMPHRENA HAAGEANA

'QIS™ Carmine' is a fabulous rose color, a glowing deep pink; grows 30 inches (75 cm) tall with 1-inch (2.5 cm) blooms.

'Strawberry Fields' is a beautiful, brilliant, sparkling red bloom that really does look like an upside-down strawberry. The brittle, branching stems make this one a challenge to harvest; grows 30 inches (75 cm) tall with 1-inch (2.5 cm) blooms.

flower farmer insider tip

The lack of support netting makes these easier to cut at the base of the plant, but efficient harvesting may still take some practice. Don't be afraid to strip off side shoots after cutting.

Grasses

Panicum elegans, 'Frosted Explosion'; *Panicum violaceum*, 'Green Drops'; *Pennisetum glaucum*, **Pearl Millet, 'Purple Majesty';** *Setaria italica*, **'Millet Lime Light', Foxtail Millet, 'Hylander', 'Lowlander'**

Grasses are always popular in landscaping, but you may be surprised to learn that some ornamental grasses are also great in bouquets and arrangements! Their vast array of forms, textures, and colors enhance our summer and fall offerings and are always popular with customers—particularly the draping varieties of ornamental grasses, which provide a sense of movement in a bouquet and a lovely naturalistic feel. One of their characteristics I appreciate is that many grasses have a potentially long window of harvest.

Although most grasses used in landscapes naturalize and become perennial in the right conditions, the varieties of ornamental grass we grow are all considered tender annuals. In fact, there is one we succession plant every week right

flower farmer insider tip

Our favorite varieties are all great to sell either fresh or dried. They make fantastic filler for fall wreaths as well.

alongside our sunflowers. Beyond that weekly planting, I include other varieties in later successions to be the new additions in late-summer and fall bouquets. I especially love bouquets of all the grasses that are beautiful fresh and easy to dry. Grasses are drought tolerant, attract birds, and are also beautiful either as cut flowers, left out in the landscape, or on your patio.

Transplant to the garden when 3 to 5 inches tall.

growing facts

Preferred season: Warm

Starting from seed:
- Prefer to start seed indoors
- Start seed indoors 3 to 4 weeks before planting outdoors
- Prefer to start in ¾-inch (2 cm) soil blocks
- Needs need darkness to sprout; cover lightly with soil
- Soil temperature: 70 to 75°F (21 to 24°C)
- 5 to 14 days to sprout
- Air temperature for optimal transplant growth: 75 to 90°F (24 to 32°C)
- Transplant to the garden when: 4 inches (10 cm) tall

Sun requirements: Minimum 8 hours, more is better

Height: 24 to 60 inches (60 to 150 cm)

Rows of plants per 36-inch (90 cm)-wide bed: Varies, see following

Plant spacing in row: 6 inches (15 cm)

Days to bloom: Varies, see following

Flower support: No

Fertilization: Standard bed preparation (see page 57)

home garden tip

Ornamental grasses are not only great in landscaping, but also in containers as cut flowers. Experiment with adding them to mixed plantings in containers as a backdrop, or in a large single clump for more of an architectural feel.

- **Seeding and growing tips:** We sow these in ¾-inch (2 cm) soil blocks, just very lightly covered with soil (about ⅛ inch [0.3 cm]). We prefer to start seeds indoors, and pinching is not necessary or encouraged with grasses. Make the cut at ground level to encourage new growth.

- **Flower support notes:** Not recommended

- **Harvesting and conditioning notes:** Make the harvest cut at ground level. Strip lower leaves to remove excess stem bulk, taking extra care not to break the stems. Follow the standard conditioning steps on page 32. Expect stems to last 7 to 10 days in the vase, or up to 1 year dried at the proper stage. Ornamental grasses are easily air-dried, either hung upside-down for upright forms or bunched in vases for draping ones. Grasses do not require or benefit from cooler storage.

- **Good to know:** Reseeding is common in some growing conditions, but should not be relied on for cut-flower production.

Favorite Varieties

Plant close with eight rows across a 36-inch (90 cm)-wide bed and 6 inches (15 cm) apart in the row unless otherwise noted.

Do Not Pinch

PANICUM ELEGANS
'Frosted Explosion' is a wonderful bouquet filler and topper with light and airy plumes with sparkles on the tips. Harvest as the plumes are just emerging; 90 to 110 days to maturity; grows 24 to 32 inches (60 to 80 cm) tall.

PANICUM VIOLACEUM

'Green Drops' has unique, loose-hanging tassels of bright green that age to shades of red, purple, and gold. Harvest time depends on which color tassels you're after; use at any stage and also dried; 65 to 75 days to maturity; grows 36 to 48 inches (90 to 120 cm) tall.

PENNISETUM GLAUCUM

'Purple Majesty Millet' is a corn-like plant that has purple foliage with cattail-like spikes. Harvest stems as they are emerging from the foliage or after the pollen stage (looks like yellow-white specs all over the head). Plant four rows across a 36-inch (90 cm)-wide bed and 6 inches (15 cm) apart in the row; 120 days to maturity; grows 36 to 60 inches (90 to 150 cm) tall.

SETARIA ITALICA

'Hylander', 'Lowlander' offers slightly different head shapes and a lovely bronze tone for later in the season; 60 to 70 days to maturity; grows 36 to 48 inches (90 to 120 cm) tall.

'Lime Light Millet' has a long window of harvest from when the fuzzy lime-green head just begins to emerge until the more developed seed head starts to drape. I succession plant weekly alongside our ProCut™ sunflowers because their days to maturity are similar. I harvest two or three grass stems from a single plant before this combination bed is pulled to prepare for the next planting; 60 to 70 days to maturity; grows 36 to 48 inches (90 to 120 cm) tall.

RIGHT, FROM TOP *From left to right: 'Green Drops', 'Limelight Millet', 'Purple Majesty', 'Highlander', 'Explosion Grass', and 'Lowlander.'*

Grasses are beautiful in the garden, used fresh and dried. 'Purple Majesty Millet' front and 'Lime Light Millet' back.

Helianthus annus

Sunflower

Sunflowers are a favorite and have held a spot in our top-ten bestselling cut flowers and seeds for years. Add variety to your harvest throughout the season by changing up the varieties and colors in your succession planting plan. Go with light colors in spring, bright colors in summer, and dark colors in fall. My favorites follow, but I'm always testing more to see which ones I'll love next! Sunflowers can be an extremely dependable crop, so much so that we were able to fund the purchase of my tractor from a single year's sunflower crop profits!

One of the unknown beneficial characteristics of single-stemmed sunflowers is that you can control their bloom size with the spacing between the plants in the garden. The close 6-inch (15 cm) or less spacing I recommend produces the perfect 4-inch (10 cm) blooms

growing facts

Preferred season: Warm

Starting from seed:

- Prefer to start seed indoors; can also be sown in the garden
- Start seed indoors 2 to 3 weeks before planting outdoors
- Prefer to start in plastic 128-cell plug trays or 2-inch (5 cm) soil blocker
- Needs darkness to sprout; cover with soil
- Soil temperature: 70°F (21°C)
- 2 to 7 days to sprout
- Air temperature for optimal transplant growth: 75 to 90°F (24 to 32° C)
- Transplant to the garden when: 3 to 5 inches (7.5 to 13 cm) tall

Sun requirement: Minimum 8 hours, more is better

Height: Varies, 3 to 8 feet (0.9 to 2.4 m)

Rows of plants per 36-inch (90 cm)-wide bed: 6 for single stem, 2 for branching

Plant spacing in row: 6 inches (15 cm) for single stem, 12 inches (30 cm) for branching

Days to bloom: 55 to 110, depending on variety

Flower support: Yes

Fertilization: Standard bed preparation (see page 57); additional field applications are beneficial

'Sunfill™': Green sunflowers are often grown for their voluptuous buds as a filler for bouquets to use before they even develop and open.

for the best cut flowers, but you can also space that same variety farther apart in the garden and grow a larger bloom. Most modern hybrid cut-flower varieties are bred to be pollenless to improve vase life and avoid pollen dropping on tabletops and other flowers in a bouquet. The pollinators still love them because they do produce nectar, just not pollen.

- **Seeding and growing tips:** I have great results transplanting sunflowers. The pest and weed pressure in my gardens made direct sowing undependable and frustrating. When starting lots of seeds each week, use 128 cell plug trays to start; if starting fewer seeds, I use the 2-inch (5 cm) soil block maker. Sunflowers germinate more quickly and grow a stronger root system when placed on a seedling heat mat. Once 50 percent has sprouted, move the tray from the heat mat to the grow light or outdoors in full sun if temperatures are above 70°F (21°C). When I place trays

LEFT, FROM TOP *Stage to harvest: Harvest when the first petals begin opening and lifting off the center of the flower. Blooms will continue to open indoors protected from pest and weather damage. Sunflower 'Rouge Royale.'*

Sunflower harvest hack: Strip all stem foliage except the top single leaf before cutting the stems. Wearing gloves and holding the sunflower bloom with one hand, slide the other hand down the stem stripping all but the very top one leaf. Cut and gather the stems.

flower farmer insider tip

Succession plant sunflowers weekly for a consistent supply. Because sunflower transplants tolerate cool weather, I will gamble and start seeds earlier and later to get blooms sooner and later in the season. The first seeds are started 6 weeks before the last expected spring frost to be planted outdoors with hoops and lightweight row covers for protection when 3 weeks old. The last seeding is done about 50 days before the first expected fall frost in hopes that the frost will come late. These gamble plantings can bloom during the highest demand times for flowers. Start at least a portion of the same variety and color of seeds each week for a timely weekly harvest as different colors within a variety can vary in days to bloom.

of young sunflower seedlings outdoors on the porch, I provide protection from hungry birds and rabbits by covering the trays with lightweight row cover. Transplants are ready to plant in the garden when 2 to 3 weeks old, and the transplant can be pulled easily from the cell by the stem. Sunflowers tend to become lanky, tangled, and generally suffer if left in the tray beyond 3 weeks. Rotate where you plant sunflowers from year to year to keep potential pests and diseases in check.

- **Flower support notes:** Although their stems are sturdy enough for calm, mild conditions, sunflowers benefit from netting during storms and windy conditions. Netting is particularly essential for gardeners and smaller farms, where stem losses have a bigger impact. When I was in high-production planting 1,200+ sunflowers per week, I didn't

have the time or resources to net them, so I had to be okay with potentially losing some of them in bad weather.

- **Harvesting and conditioning notes:** See Stage to harvest image (page 202). Sunflowers continue to open after cutting, so harvest at a very early stage to help protect the petals from drying winds, hungry pests that chew the petals, and others that soil the flowers. To prolong vase life and help prevent drooping heads, leave only the top leaf on the stem. When harvesting single-stemmed varieties, cut to any length, with 24 inches (60 cm) of stem sufficient for most uses. Branching-variety stems should be cut at the base of the stem to encourage more branching. Sunflowers are one of the "Dirty Dozen Flowers" (see page 33 for details), so follow the standard conditioning steps on page 32, including the chlorine tablet in the harvest bucket. Expect flowers to last 7 to 9 days in the vase. Cut stems can be stored in a cooler at 36 to 41°F (2 to 5°C) to slow bloom opening, or stored in warm conditions so they open sooner. If your flower heads are drooping (more common in some colors than others), it is typically from a lack of hydration. We find that using Quick Dip according to the package directions helps.

- **Good to know:** Do not pinch single-stem variety sunflowers even though some varieties may occasionally produce side shoots with blooms. I find that only the center stem is usable as a good cut flower. Branching varieties benefit from pinching to encourage strong branching from the base of the plant and to produce longer stems. Pinch back to four leaves once the plant reaches 12 to 18 inches (30 to 45 cm) tall.

Favorite Varieties

Single Stem, Do Not Pinch

'Marley' features bicolor petals in shades of lemon yellow, with plum and burgundy tones and is a beautiful addition to fall bouquets and arrangements. This is my favorite among bicolor sunflowers because it is pollenless and has great vase life, holding onto its petals longer than other bicolor varieties. Expect 5 to 10 days to sprout, 55 to 65 days to bloom; grows 48 to 72 inches (120 to 180 cm) tall.

home garden tip

Sunflowers can also be grown in containers, grow bags, and even in kiddie pools with drainage holes added! The volume of soil in the container and the number of seedlings planted in will affect the height of the plants and the bloom size, so experiment to find the combination that is best for your container.

LEFT, FROM TOP *Sunflower transplants grown in a 128-plug tray ready to be planted in the garden at 3-weeks-old.*

A real favorite from the 'ProCuts™' series is 'Horizon.' It is the classic sunflower orange petal with the brown disc, but most of its blooms face upward instead of outward. They fill that hole in the top of bouquets. Brilliant!

'ProCuts'™ is the sunflower series I grew during the high-production years. In fact, I only grew one color, ProCut™ 'Orange', because it was a strong producer and was in high demand. In recent years, I've started growing other colors in this series and find them all to be great additions to bouquets. ProCut™ comes in many colors: orange, white lite, white nite, gold lite, red, bicolors, brilliance, lemon, peach, and plum. There is even a superspecial one called 'Horizon', which is orange, but with the blooms facing upward for easy use in bouquets. All ProCuts™ are pollenless, ranging from 55 to 70 days to bloom, and they continue to grow and bloom even as days get shorter in fall; grows 60 to 72 inches (150 to 180 cm) tall.

'SunFill' ™ is what I grow to use as a filler in bouquets rather than a focal flower. The

205

numerous rows of thick green sepals that come before the bloom have a succulent-like appearance, making an easy filler that can be succession planted for weekly harvests. I grow both green and purple, using the green in spring and summer and the purple in fall. Harvest the stem when the buds are full but before flowering to add a fantastic accent texture to arrangements. Blooms are pollenless and quick to mature at 50 to 55 days or less; grows 60 to 72 inches (150 to 180 cm) tall.

'Vincent' is pollenless and day-length neutral, and it features slightly rounded petals in a delightful overlapping array, producing a semi-double appearance. We grow both Vincent's Fresh with bright-green centers and Vincent's

Choice with dark-brown centers. Both are 50 to 60 days to bloom; grows 60 to 72 inches (150 to 180 cm) tall.

Branching: Pinch
(see "Pinching Plants," page 53)

'Lemonade' has fluffy lemon-yellow petals on double blooms with a green center on nice strong stems. It is stunning in the garden and in bouquets. This variety produces minimal pollen. It takes a bit longer to bloom than my other favorites at 85 to 95 days; grows 60 to 72 inches (150 to 180 cm) tall.

'Rouge Royale' is known as the chocolate sunflower! This pollenless plant can grow to a towering 80 inches (200 cm) and is covered with beautiful 3- to 4-inch (7.5 to 10 cm) dark blooms. Flower heads develop into tasty treats for the birds, who love the black oil seeds! Expect 5 to 14 days to germinate; grows 60 to 72 inches (150 to 180 cm) tall.

The ProCut™ series has been my go to sunflowers. They are quick to grow from seed to bloom, they are great cut flowers, and there are 13 colors.

Hibiscus acetosella

Hibiscus 'Mahogany Splendor'

Growing plenty of foliage is a piece of bouquet making that is so often an afterthought. Making a bouquet with beautiful flowers gets easier when there is a nice nest of interesting foliage to poke the flowers into. I learned about the important role foliage played when selling to florists. Anytime I offered foliage, they took it all. They knew having a diverse selection made richer bouquets and arrangements, plus it made the job easier. And then I met 'Mahogany Splendor' hibiscus. Such a great addition!

You're probably most familiar with hibiscus as a potted patio plant, with beautiful showy flowers. Unfortunately, those blooms don't last once cut, so they can't be used in bouquets. However, there is one variety of hibiscus that has established itself in the cut-flower market—not for its flowers but for its beautiful foliage. That is 'Mahogany Splendor'.

flower farmer insider tip

Hibiscus does not benefit from refrigeration, and it is not recommended to store hibiscus for any length of time at lower than 40°F (4°C).

A fast-growing annual that has a strong branching habit. I plant two rows in a 30-inch-wide bed and pinch the young plants to get branching started.

Also known as the cranberry hibiscus, African rosemallow, red-leaf hibiscus, or maroon mallow, hibiscus 'Mahogany Splendor' may be considered a perennial in tropical and subtropical climates, but we grow it as an annual. It produces many long stems of burgundy or maroon foliage, with jagged-edged leaves that look similar to a Japanese maple. I love it as a stark color contrast to the orange and yellow hues of late-summer and fall flowers, but it also looks great with pink flowers, white flowers, and other foliage in lime green or silver shades.

- **Seeding and growing tips:** Hibiscus is a strong sprouter that needs darkness to germinate, so push the seed deeper into the ¾-inch (2 cm) soil blocks to cover it about ⅛ inch (0.3 cm) deep. It prefers humid and hot weather, so wait until all danger of frost has passed before planting out. Hibiscus

transplants benefit particularly from the soil-warming effect of a dark-colored mulch covering such as biodegradable film, black-side up. This hibiscus can be grown in partial shade, but beware that the deep burgundy color will not develop—it will look more green instead—and this is definitely a way for growers to grow more variation. Hibiscus grows naturally as a single

home garden tip

Hibiscus can also be grown as a backdrop to bright summer and fall flowers in landscape plantings or in large containers. Mass plantings resemble a shrub that can be used as a seasonal hedge and you can snip it some for bouquets.

main stem but can be pinched to encourage branching. However, make sure your season is long enough to wait for those branches to grow enough to cut, which is around 6 weeks.

- **Flower support notes:** Not recommended. Stems get woody as they mature, making the plant pretty sturdy even as it grows quite tall.

- **Harvesting and conditioning notes:** See Stage to harvest photo (page 209). Hibiscus should be well hydrated before cutting. Make the cut at the base of the stem (see illustration: Where to Make the Cut on Branching Annuals, page 30). Harvest when leaves are fully developed and stems are slightly woody. Do not wait for flower buds to form. Strip off all leaves that will not be used in your design or bouquet, leaving mainly the top leaves. Hibiscus is prone to wilting, so harvest very early in the day and immediately move it to a cool area for conditioning. You may notice that your harvest bucket water turns red—that is sap from the freshly cut stems. Follow the standard conditioning steps on page 32. Hibiscus benefits from the use of holding solution. Expect stems to last roughly 7 days in the vase. Hibiscus does not dry well, nor does it require or benefit from cooler storage.

- **Good to know:** A single hibiscus plant can produce many stems. In the home garden, just a few plants would provide several stems a week in late summer and fall for bouquets.

growing facts

Preferred season: Warm

Starting from seed:
- Prefer to start seed indoors
- Start seed indoors 4 to 5 weeks before planting outdoors
- Prefer to start in ¾-inch (2 cm) soil blocks
- Needs darkness to sprout; cover lightly with soil
- Soil temperature: 70°F (21°C)
- 3 to 5 days to sprout
- Air temperature for optimal transplant growth: 75 to 90°F (24 to 32°C)
- Transplant to the garden when: 3 to 5 inches (7.5 to 13 cm) tall

Sun requirements: Minimum 8 hours, more is better

Height: 36 to 60 inches (990 to 150 cm)

Rows of plants per 36-inch (90 cm)-wide bed: 2

Plant spacing in row: 12 inches (30 cm)

Days to bloom: 115 to 130 (harvest before bloom, see following)

Flower support: No

Fertilization: Standard bed preparation (see page 57); additional field applications are beneficial

FROM FAR LEFT *Stage to harvest: Allow the tips to fully develop before cutting. A beautiful group of plants growing on Wind Haven Farm, King William, VA.*

Hibiscus seedlings ready for the garden as they are pushing past 5 inches. Growing in the ¾-inch soil block.

Ocimum basilicum, Ocimum basilicum var. *citriodora*

Basil

You may already know about basil's wide use as a culinary herb, particularly popular in Mediterranean cooking. But it is also a fantastically fragrant and beautiful addition to bouquets and arrangements, one that we've used since the very beginning at our farm. There are more than thirty-five recognized species and varieties of basil, and more are developed each year.

home garden tip

Growing basil in pots and planters is easy and a great way to control the light and moisture received, which you may want to adjust throughout the season. Remember to harvest stems weekly to keep new shoots coming all season long.

Several varieties of basil hold up as a cut flower filler to add the perfect touch of fragrance to summer and fall bouquets. No question that the all-time favorite is Mrs. Burns' Lemon Basil for its fragrance of just-cut lemon, plus its light-green color fits any bouquet. I also grow a few other basil varieties, changing it up with different scents and colors as the season progresses. This gives lots of variation in bouquets without extra fuss as they all have virtually the same growing requirements.

- **Seeding and growing tips:** Basil prefers darkness to germinate, pushing the seed a little deeper into the ¾-inch (2 cm) soil blocks will provide the required cover. Basil does not like cool temperatures and can sustain damage at 50°F (10°C), so I

ABOVE, FROM FAR LEFT *Cinnamon basil at the stage to harvest as the flower is elongating*

Transplant to the garden when 3 to 5 inches tall. 'Mrs. Burn's Lemon Basil' growing in ¾-inch soil blocker ready for the garden.

growing facts

Preferred season: Warm

Starting from seed:

- Prefer to start seed indoors; can also be sown in the garden
- Start seed indoors 4 to 6 weeks before planting outdoors
- Prefer to start in ¾-inch (2 cm) soil blocks (see tips following)
- Needs darkness to sprout; cover lightly with soil
- Soil temperature: 70°F (21°C)
- 5 to 10 days to sprout
- Air temperature for optimal transplant growth: 75 to 90°F (24 to 32°C)
- Transplant to the garden when: 3 to 5 inches (7.5 to 13 cm) tall

Sun requirement: Minimum 8 hours, more is better

Height: 20 to 30 inches (50 to 75 cm)

Rows of plants per 36-inch (90 cm)-wide bed: 4

Plant spacing in row: 6 inches (15 cm)

Days to bloom: 85 to 100

Flower support: Yes

Fertilization: Standard bed preparation (see page 57)

wait until all danger of frost is passed before planting out. Basil prefers moist soil for the best production and is prone to stress in high heat. Plan to irrigate regularly, particularly in the heat of summer. In very hot, dry climates, it may do best with some afternoon shade.

- **Flower support notes:** Installing support netting is beneficial to support the tall branching stems.

- **Harvesting and conditioning notes:** See Stage to harvest image (page 210). Make the cut at the base of the stem (see illustration: Where to Make the Cut on Branching Annuals, page 30). Start harvesting stems as the first blooms begin to open at the bottom of the flower. Leave only the foliage on the top 4 inches (10 cm) or so of the stem—stripping off all the lower leaves is important to prevent wilting. The remaining leaves are what will be seen in the bouquet and provide fragrance. Follow the standard conditioning steps on page 32. When harvested at the appropriate stage, expect stems to last 7 days. Do not put in a cooler.

- **Good to know:** All varieties of basil can be used in cooking; however, do not use stems for cooking that have been treated as cut flowers as the chemicals used for this purpose are not approved for human consumption.

Top left and around: 'Purple Ruffles,' 'Cardinal,' 'Cinnamon,' and 'Mrs. Burn's Lemon'

flower farmer insider tip

Particularly early in the season, you may want to pinch only half of your seedlings for a jump start on your succession planting plans. As your season length allows, we recommend succession planting monthly for continuous harvest. Basil turns black if refrigerated. If selling to florists and supermarkets, advise them to store it at room temperature, not in the cooler.

Favorite Varieties

Pinch All
(see "Pinching Plants," page 53)

OCIMUM BASILICUM

'Cardinal' has a whopper bloom that is the star in this variety. Large, densely packed reddish-purple flowers are suspended atop plants with burgundy stems and bright-green leaves, making this basil striking and fragrant; grows to 30 inches (75 cm) tall.

'Cinnamon' adds a spicy cinnamon scent to bouquets. Stems are a deep purple with lavender blooms, creating a nice visual contrast; grows 24 to 30 inches (60 to 75 cm) tall with 2-inch (5 cm) leaves.

'Purple Ruffles' is a dark red ruffle-leafed basil that is great filler foliage to accent the bright oranges and yellows in your late-summer or early fall palette, such as zinnias, sunflowers, and marigolds; grows to 30 inches (75 cm) tall.

OCIMUM BASILICUM VAR. CITRIODORA

'Mrs. Burns' Lemon' has a lemon scent. I recommend rustling the seedlings, garden plants, and especially bouquets when you pass by to delight the senses. Its long 2½-inch (6 cm) leaves are bright green with white blooms. This basil is our top pick; grows 20 to 30 inches (50 to 75 cm) tall.

Ornamentals

Cucurbita pepo var. *ovifera*, **Gourd Vine**; *Cardiospermum halicacabum*, **Love-in-a Puff Vine**; *Dolichos lablab*, **Hyacinth Bean Vine**; *Gomphocarpus physocarpus*, **Hairy Balls**; *Solanum integrifolium*, **Pumpkin-on-a-Stick**; *Solanum aethiopicum* var. *gilo*, **Striped Garden Egg**

The plants in this section are really special, fun to grow, and generate a lot of interest in bouquets, large installations for weddings or events, and are even sold to florists. You'll notice that none is really grown for the flowers. Instead, the fruit or seedpods steal the show. Experiment with one or all of these in your garden or on your farm!

- **Seeding and growing tips:** The timing of seed starting is an important planning aspect for these crops, as some of them may only be in peak demand during a short seasonal window. Note the days to bloom or maturity and then backtrack to determine when you need to start seeds to begin harvesting before your target use or sale date. You'll notice that we use the larger 2-inch (5 cm) soil blocks for a couple of these, which means you'll need a lot more soil-blocking mix per seed, so plan accordingly.

Cucurbita pepo var. *ovifera*
Spinning Gourd

Spinning gourds are tiny, precious decorative gourds that can be used either fresh or cured. They are 2 to 3 inches (5 to 7.5 cm) long and green with white or light-green stripes. To support them, we create a tunnel out of metal livestock panels, then plant seedlings in a raised

growing facts

Preferred season: Warm

Starting from seed:
- Prefer to start seeds indoors
- Start seed indoors 2 to 3 weeks before planting outdoors
- Prefer to start in 2-inch (5 cm) soil blocks
- Needs darkness to sprout; cover with soil
- Soil temperature: 70°F (21°C)
- 7 to 10 days to sprout
- Air temperature for optimal transplant growth: 75 to 90°F (24 to 32°C)
- Transplant to the garden when: 5 to 8 inches (13 to 20 cm) tall

Sun requirement: Minimum 8 hours, more is better

Height: 8 to 12 feet (2.4 to 3.6 m)

Rows of plants per 36-inch (90 cm)-wide bed: Single row along support

Plant spacing in row: 12 inches (30 cm)

Days to bloom: 95

Flower support: Yes, tunnel or trellis

Fertilization: Standard bed preparation (see page 57)

WARM-SEASON TENDER ANNUALS

home garden tip

The vining plants require support structures other than the typical flower support netting. A common underestimation is the sturdiness required to support climbing vines. They are bountiful growers in one season and get heavy when they begin to bloom and set seedpods. To prevent having to repair a collapsed structure late in the season when the plants are most beautiful, go heavy duty from the start.

bed on both sides; see "How to Make a Support Tunnel" (page 216).

To cure gourds, leave them on the vine until dried, but remove before frost. Place them in a dry, warm, well-ventilated area on a bed of paper, not touching each other. It's not unusual for the gourds to get moldy as they dry, but if any start to get soft or cave in, that's a sign of rot and those gourds should be discarded. Once the shell hardens, clean if needed by soaking in water for 10 to 15 minutes followed by a vigorous scrubbing.

Cardiospermum halicacabum
Love-in-a-Puff

Love-in-a-puff is a delicate-looking but vigorously growing vine. It produces green seedpods that are a beautiful addition to arrangements or event installations. The round black seeds have a little white heart shape on them, lending "love" to the common name. This vine grows multiple stems that can become tangled; thin as

LEFT *From left to right: 1. Pumpkin on a stick 2. Spinning gourd 3. Hairy balls 4. Hyacinth Bean vine 5. Love-in-a-puff 6. Striped garden egg*

needed and guide vines to grow straight up the support for easier harvesting. Pods develop after the tiny white blooms and can be used when green or brown. Harvest vines early in the day to prevent wilting. Cut at the base of the vine and gently pull it away from the support structure. Expect vine foliage and pods to last 7 to 10 days.

growing facts

Preferred season: Warm

Starting from seed:
- Prefer to start seeds indoors
- Start seed indoors 3 to 4 weeks before planting outdoors
- Prefer to start in 2-inch (5 cm) soil blocks
- Needs darkness to sprout; cover with soil
- Soil temperature: 70°F (21°C)
- 5 to 10 days to sprout
- Air temperature for optimal transplant growth: 75 to 90°F (24 to 32°C)
- Transplant to the garden when: 3 to 5 inches (7.5 to 13 cm) tall

Sun requirements: Minimum 8 hours, more is better

Height: 8 to 10 feet (2.4 to 3 m)

Rows of plants per 36-inch (90 cm)-wide bed: Single row along support

Plant spacing in row: 12 inches (30 cm)

Days to maturity: 120

Flower support: Yes, tunnel or trellis

Fertilization: Standard bed preparation (see page 57)

how to make a support tunnel

SUPPLIES

- Livestock panels (ours are 4 feet wide × 16 feet long [1.2 × 4.8 m])
- Strong metal rebar stakes 4-feet (1.2 m) long; 3 stakes per side of the panel
- Heavy-duty cable ties to secure panels to stakes
- Sledgehammer or fence post driver

Drive 2 or 3 stakes into the ground on each side of the proposed tunnel. Bend the flexible panel and place it between the stakes so it forms an arch. Cable tie the panel to the stakes. If building a multipanel tunnel, cable tie the panels together as well.

We made raised beds that run along the outside edge of both sides of the tunnel. Mulch the inside of the tunnel deeply and plant on the outside edge.

ABOVE *Love-in-a-puff vines with the green seed pods attached make long-lasting unique cutflowers. The challenge is cutting often enough to keep it from tangling.*

Dolichos lablab
Hyacinth Bean Vine, 'Ruby Moon'

Hyacinth bean is a real stunner with its purple stems, beautiful sweet pea–like blooms, and 2- to 3-inch (5 to 7.5 cm) magenta beans! The flowers have a short vase life but are nice for events; the seedpod stage holds for 7 days. My nickname for this plant is "Jack and the Beanstalk" because of its vigorous growth. A favorite of bees and hummingbirds!

growing facts

Preferred season: Warm

Starting from seed:
- Prefer to start seeds indoors
- Start seed indoors 2 to 3 weeks before planting outdoors
- Prefer to start in 2-inch (5 cm) soil blocks
- Needs darkness to sprout; cover with soil
- Soil temperature: 70°F (21°C)
- 5 to 10 days to sprout
- Air temperature for optimal transplant growth: 75 to 90°F (24 to 32°C)
- Transplant to the garden when: 5 to 8 inches (13 to 20 cm) tall

Sun requirements: Minimum 8 hours, more is better

Height: 8 to 10 feet (2.4 to 3 m)

Rows of plants per 36-inch (90 cm)-wide bed: Single row along support

Plant spacing in row: 12 inches (30 cm)

Days to bloom: 110 to 120

Flower support: Yes, tunnel or trellis

Fertilization: Standard bed preparation (see page 57)

LEFT, FROM TOP *Hyacinth bean blooms are beautiful, but short lived. It's the bean pods that follow that make such great stems to use in fall decorations and bouquets.*

Transplant to the garden when 3 to 5 inches tall. Spinning Gourd and Hyacinth Bean Vine growing in 2-inch soil blocks because of their large seed.

217

Gomphocarpus physocarpus
Hairy Balls

Fuzzy green seedpods that grow to the size of tennis balls! Originally from southeast Africa, this member of the milkweed family is a favorite of butterflies, bees, and flower arrangers. Pinch when 10 inches (25 cm) tall to establish a more robust, branching plant. Produces an insignificant little flower that is followed by a ball-shaped seedpod. Harvest pods at any size or stage, making the harvest cut at the base of the stem. As a variety of milkweed, this plant contains a white sap that will temporarily seep from the cut and where the leaves are stripped, so it is recommended to wear gloves when handling. The plants may attract aphids, which can be sprayed off the plants easily with a stream of water from a hose or shaken off the stem during harvest.

LEFT Fall is when I plan for most of the ornamentals to be ready for harvest. I am holding Hairy Ball stems, with Love-in-a-Puff and Hyacinth Bean growing on a tunnel behind me.

growing facts

Preferred season: Warm

Starting from seed:
- Prefer to start seeds indoors
- Start seed indoors 4 to 6 weeks before planting outdoors
- Prefer to start in ¾-inch (2 cm) soil blocks
- Needs darkness to sprout; cover with soil
- Soil temperature: 70°F (21°C)
- 14 to 21 days to sprout
- Air temperature for optimal transplant growth: 75 to 90°F (24 to 32°C)
- Transplant to the garden when: 3 to 5 inches (7.5 to 13 cm) tall

Sun requirements: Minimum 8 hours, more is better

Height: 5 feet (1.5 m)

Rows of plants per 36-inch (90 cm)-wide bed: 2

Plant spacing in row: 12 inches (30 cm)

Days to maturity: 90 to 120

Flower support: No

Fertilization: Standard bed preparation (see page 48)

flower farmer insider tip

Most of these plants can be harvested at multiple stages, depending on your use or your selling outlet. Pumpkin-on-a-stick can be harvested with green eggplants, or you can wait until they turn orange. I prefer to harvest hairy balls when the seedpods are 1 inch (2.5 cm) or so for use in bouquets, or wait until they're bigger to use in installations. If selling to florists, keep in mind that different florists may want these items at varying stages of development as well. These stems do not require or benefit from cooler storage.

Solanaceae, Solanum integrifolium, Solanum aethiopicum var. *gilo*
Pumpkin-on-a-Stick, Striped Garden Egg

The ornamental eggplant varieties are anticipated all season for the whimsy they add to fall bouquets. These plants grow long, sturdy stems with miniature 1- to 3-inch (2.5 to 7.5 cm) eggplants that resemble pumpkins and eggs. The plants can be pinched to encourage branching and additional fruit production. Beware, they are thorny plants! Harvest when green and immature or as the fruit ripens by cutting stems at the base and stripping off all foliage and thorns. Use fresh or dried, on the stem, or cut off to use individually.

I use Pumpkin-on-a-Stick in the green stage in bouquets and sometimes pick the lower fruits to use for table decorations. Fruit will develop near the top of the stems later in the season.

growing facts

Preferred season: Warm

Starting from seed:
- Prefer to start seeds indoors
- Start seed indoors 4 to 6 weeks before planting outdoors
- Prefer to start in ¾-inch (2 cm) soil blocks
- Needs darkness to sprout; cover with soil
- Soil temperature: 70°F (21°C)
- 10 to 20 days to sprout
- Air temperature for optimal transplant growth: 75 to 90°F (24 to 32°)
- Transplant to the garden when: 3 to 5 inches (7.5 to 13 cm) tall

Sun requirements: Minimum 8 hours, more is better

Height: 36 to 48 inches (90 to 120 cm)

Rows of plants per 36-inch (90 cm)-wide bed: 2

Plant spacing in row: 24 inches (60 cm)

Days to maturity: 65 to 90

Flower support: Yes, flower support netting

Fertilization: Standard bed preparation (see page 57)

Tagetes erecta

Marigold

Cut-flower varieties of marigolds are gigantic! The blooms are huge and the plants are tall—they are not the common marigolds found in landscapes and containers. I always include them in my gardens because they are such strong growers and have such a long vase life. Their bold, vibrant colors make them perfect for summer bouquets, plus they bloom right up until the first fall frost. The newer gold and white buttercream–colored marigolds have become staples in my fall bouquets and decorations.

There are exciting new varieties that have broadened the color range of marigolds, plus some have low to no fragrance, which makes them even more versatile, so I include even more of them in my garden. Marigolds are traditionally known to have a strong scent, but few know it is the foliage, not the flower, that smells. For cut-flower usage, strip off all the leaves to greatly reduce the scent.

- **Seeding and growing tips:** I start marigolds in ¾-inch (2 cm) soil blocks, though at first it may seem like they're too big. As with zinnias, poke the pointed end of the seed into the block, leaving the "tail" to protrude

home garden tip

Including marigolds in later succession plantings can help you miss out on Japanese beetle season and the damage that ensues.

ABOVE *Marigolds are a staple on our farm. If anyone had a problem with the fragrance, we offered to remove the foliage that eliminates it. From left to right: 'Coco' orange, gold, yellow, and 'Nosento.'*

growing facts

Preferred season: Warm

Starting from seed:
- Prefer to start seed indoors
- Start seed indoors 4 to 6 weeks before planting outdoors
- Prefer to start in ¾-inch (2 cm) soil blocks
- Needs darkness to sprout; cover lightly with soil
- Soil temperature: 70 to 75°F (21 to 24°C)
- 2 to 7 days to sprout
- Air temperature for optimal transplant growth: 75 to 90°F (24 to 32°C)
- Transplant to the garden when: 3 to 5 inches (7.5 to 13 cm) tall

Sun requirement: Minimum 8 hours, more is better

Height: 24 to 42 inches (60 to 105 cm)

Rows of plants per 36-inch (90 cm)-wide bed: 4

Plant spacing in row: 6 inches (15 cm)

Days to bloom: 75 to 90

Flower support: Yes

Fertilization: Standard bed preparation (see page 57); additional field applications are beneficial

from the top of the block, if necessary. This gives the seed the cover and darkness it needs to germinate. I start it 3 to 4 weeks before planting out. Plant seedlings slightly deeper in the soil because additional roots will form along the lower part of the stem, resulting in a sturdier plant. Start additional plants by rooting the pinched-off stems in water, which quickly develop plants.

- **Flower support notes:** Installing support netting is beneficial to support the giant, heavy blooms.

- **Harvesting and conditioning notes:** Harvest at any stage of opening; blooms will not open further after cutting. I love the more immature blooms with green in the middle (see illustration: Where to Make the Cut on Branching Annuals, page 30). Marigolds are one of the "Dirty Dozen Flowers" (see page 33 for details). Follow the standard conditioning steps on page 32, including the chlorine tablet. Expect stems to last 10 to 14 days and even to develop roots in the vase.

- **Good to know:** Marigolds are a good trap crop for Japanese beetles. I visit our patch each morning in beetle season armed with soapy water in a jar. I place it under the blooms and tap the flower to help them drop into the soapy water, then dispose of them. The light-colored marigolds with low fragrance seem to be the most attractive to and heavily damaged by Japanese beetles.

Favorite Varieties

Pinch All
(see "Pinching Plants," page 53)

'Coco' has fully double blooms that come in deep orange, gold, and yellow. I grow all three colors to add texture to fall bouquets. This gold is a real favorite, with 2½- to 3-inch (6 to 7.5 cm) blooms; grows 36 inches (90 cm) tall.

'Giant' produces large flower heads on strong stems. I love both the yellow and the orange for fresh bouquets, and they are gorgeous in the

garden with their voluptuous 3-inch (7.5 cm) blooms; grows 36 inches (90 cm) tall.

'Nosento Limegreen' is nearly scentless, which makes it an excellent option for those sensitive to the fragrance. It has fully double blooms in shades from lime green in the center to lemon yellow as it opens and develops its 2- to 3-inch (5 to 7.5 cm) blooms; grows 24 to 36 inches (60 to 90 cm) tall.

'White Swan' produces fully double, buttercream white blooms with a milder fragrance than typical marigolds. This color is a mustgrow in any season, with its 2- to 3-inch (5 to 7.5 cm) blooms; grows as a more compact plant, 28 to 36 inches (70 to 90 cm) tall.

ABOVE, FROM LEFT *Transplant seedlings to the garden when 3 to 5 inches tall. They don't all get planted on time.*

Stage to harvest: Cut as soon as the bloom is big enough to contribute up until full open. I harvest blooms earlier than later because I like the green in the center. 'White Swan' marigolds are a buttercream color and have low fragrance.

flower farmer insider tip

Marigolds are in high demand as fresh-cut flowers. Along with sunflowers and celosia they were a staple ingredient in my grocery store account's mixed bouquets because of how well they held up. They are also great dried, holding their color beautifully. Now with low- to no-fragrance varieties, they are even more useful.

223

Zinnia elegans

Zinnia

Hands down, zinnias are the favorite garden flower for many. As a flower farmer, it is in our top-ten bestselling cut flowers. As a retailer, we sell more zinnia seeds than any other seed. No question, we all love zinnias, and with good reason. Many remember seeing zinnias in their grandparents' garden; in fact, zinnias are the first flowers I grew and took to my grandmother weekly to enjoy. But the varieties I grow are not the same zinnias that Grandma grew. These are newer hybrid varieties bred specifically for their giant blooms and with more colors.

Zinnias come in a broad range of sizes, making them a versatile choice for focal and filler flower use. You can grow soft blushes, whites, and greens for wedding work, or bold, jewel-toned corals, purples, and orange flowers for the kitchen table bouquet. Zinnias are easy-care cut flowers that attract butterflies, birds, hummingbirds, and beneficial bugs, and are drought tolerant once established

Zinnias are so prolific that a very small patch will provide a handful of blooms a week if you harvest on a regular schedule and give them

what they want. They are known as a "cut and come again" flower because cutting the stem causes the plant to branch and produce more blooms. All varieties of zinnia respond incredibly well to pinching; I recommend pinching about 50 percent of the seedlings so you have some plants that bloom earlier with fewer stems and some that bloom later but have more stems (see "Pinching Plants," page 53).

The challenge I face growing zinnias is that they tend to get powdery mildew in our hot and humid summer weather. If you're growing in similar conditions and your space allows for it, you may find that spacing them farther apart (up to 12 inches [30 cm] apart in the row) may lessen the chance of powdery mildew by improving airflow. If and when mildew comes,

growing facts

Preferred season: Warm

Starting from seed:
- Prefer to start seed indoors; can also be sown in the garden
- Start seed indoors 2 to 3 weeks before planting outdoors
- Prefer to start in ¾-inch (2 cm) soil blocks
- Needs darkness to sprout (see seeding and growing tips following)
- Soil temperature: 70°F (21°C)
- 2 to 7 days to sprout
- Air temperature for optimal transplant growth: 75 to 90°F (24 to 32°C)
- Transplant to the garden when: 3 to 5 inches (7.5 to 13 cm) tall

Sun requirement: Minimum 8 hours, more is better

Height: 28 to 36 inches (70 to 90 cm)

Rows of plants per 36-inch (90 cm)-wide bed: 4

Plant spacing in row: 6 inches (15 cm)

Days to bloom: 75 to 90

Flower support: Yes

Fertilization: Standard bed preparation (see page 57)

CLOCKWISE FROM LEFT *Zinnias have been a bestseller for decades. They remind us of our childhood and our grandmas, what's not to love? 1. 'Oklahoma' ivory 2. 'Zowie' 3. 'Uproar Rose 4. 'Benary's Giants' 5. 'Inca Cactus' 6. 'Queen' mix.*

Zinnia seedlings should be transplanted when they reach 3 to 5 inches, which is normally at 2- to 3-weeks-old.

Family hand-me-downs make the best vases. This pitcher is one of many that belonged to mamas, grandmas, and great grandmas. The 'Queen' series' muted colors seem a perfect fit for it and for fall bouquets.

ABOVE, FROM LEFT *Stage to harvest: Cut when as fully open as you want it but before the little yellow florets around the center open. Harvesting to early in development may lead to immature soft necks.*

Zinnia seedlings transplanted into beds covered with biodegradable mulch film. Beds prepared in spring were made with the black side up to help warm the soil. Beds prepared in the heat of summer were made with the white side up to help cool the surface temperature.

it is helpful to strip foliage and throw it into the trash to help eliminate spores that can spread in the garden. We have not used any treatments for mildew. If it gets going strong on a planting, we remove the crop because we have others to harvest. This is another reason I always recommend succession planting zinnias. By the time our first planting starts to develop mildew, our second planting is coming into bloom, so we can mow down the first one and prep that soil for a different crop. That way we always have a fresh crop of zinnias to harvest.

- **Seeding and growing tips:** We sow zinnia seeds in ¾-inch (2 cm) soil blocks. The space-saving size of the ¾-inch (2 cm) blocker is what allows us to start tens of thousands of zinnia seeds each season. It may seem like they're too big, but here's a seed-starting secret: Don't start the seeds too early and leave them to outgrow their space quickly. Zinnias grow to the desired 3- to 5-inch (7.5 to 13 cm) transplant size in just 2 to 3 weeks, so plan accordingly. To plant the seed, poke the pointed end into the block, leaving the "tail" of the seed to protrude from the top of the block, if necessary. Zinnias are very quick to germinate—sometimes in just 2 days—especially when placed on a heat mat. Once about half have sprouted, move the tray from the seedling heat mat to the grow light to prevent seedlings from stretching for light. Move outdoors to harden off when nearing 2 to 3 weeks old or 3 to 5 inches (7.5 to 13 cm) tall. I do not use additional fertilizer in the field beyond my standard bed preparation. Foliar feeding, in particular, is not recommended, as it can fuel the growth of powdery mildew. Zinnias are drought tolerant once established, but regular watering (drip irrigation or hand watering at ground level) will result in the most prolific and biggest blooms. Seed saving is popular with zinnias, particularly among home gardeners, but be mindful of the fact that these are hybrid varieties, and that hybrids don't reliably produce seeds of the same bloom type or color as the parent plant (they don't typically come back "true"). We don't save seeds from zinnia plants; we always buy new seeds so we're sure of what we're growing.

- **Flower support notes:** I use flower support netting on my zinnia plantings. Install netting as soon as possible after transplanting, as these are fast growers! Netting makes the first bloom center stem cut a bit more time-consuming, as you'll need to reach underneath the netting to make the cut, but the netting is so valuable as the plants' branching increases. Reduce this issue by pinching out the center stem before planting.

- **Harvesting and conditioning notes:** See Stage to harvest image (page 226). Make the cut at the base of the stem (see illustration: Where to Make the Cut on Branching Annuals, page 30). Harvest zinnias when flowers are fully open, as they will not continue to develop after cutting. Harvest blooms for cut flowers just as the little yellow flowers (stamens) begin to develop in the center. Zinnias are a member of the "Dirty Dozen Flowers" (see page 33 for details). Follow the standard conditioning steps on page 32, including the chlorine tablet

in the harvest bucket. When harvested at the appropriate stage, expect flowers to last 7 to 10 days in the vase. Zinnias do not require or benefit from cooler storage.

- **Good to know:** White and light-colored zinnias are particularly attractive to pests and will show more pest damage (and bug poop) earlier than other colors, so they'll need to be harvested earlier in their lifecycle. Experiment with how early you can harvest them without suffering from bent or droopy necks.

Favorite Varieties

Pinch All
(see "Pinching Plants," page 53)

'Benary's Giant' are the gold standard for zinnias, the main zinnia cash crop for us in all our years of high production. This variety provides the tallest plants, the biggest blooms, and also a high percentage of voluptuous double blooms that can act as focal flowers in a bouquet or arrangement. They come in so many colors—pink, red, wine, lilac, purple, orange, coral, lime green, yellow, carmine, deep red, white, and salmon rose.

There is a 'Benary's Giant' zinnia color to go with everything; grows to 36 inches (90 cm) tall with 3- to 4-inch (7.5 to 10 cm) blooms.

'Giant Cactus' zinnias are unique due to their petal shape, which is meant to resemble the pointy quills of a cactus. Their fully double blooms vary in size and include several colors, such as red, purple, pink, orange, and yellow; grows 36 inches (90 cm) tall with 3 - to 6-inch (7.5 to 15 cm) blooms.

'Oklahoma' zinnias are a great complement to 'Benary's', with similar-height plants but much smaller blooms. You will get a nice mix of dainty singles and fully double blooms in colors of white, yellow, scarlet, salmon, pink, and carmine with this variety. These zinnias work great as a filler flower in bouquets; grows to 36 inches (90 cm) tall with 1½-inch (3.5 cm) blooms.

'Queen' series of zinnia is known for its gorgeous and unique soft colors, and is a favorite for wedding work in particular, but are also great in bouquets. These plants are slightly shorter and produce mostly fully double or semi-double blooms, typically in between the sizes of 'Oklahoma' and 'Benary's', and in some fabulously popular colors: lime, orange, orange blush, red lime, lemon peach, lime orange, and lime blotch. You'll want to grow them all;

home garden tip

If the length of your warm season allows for it, consider growing at least two successions of zinnias. In spring, grow pastels and light colors; in summer and fall, grow brighter and deeper colors.

grows 28 to 32 inches (70 to 80 cm) tall with 2-inch (5 cm) blooms.

'Uproar™ Rose' is a magnificent magenta pink with an almost electric neon glow. This is one of the most prolific zinnias I have grown in a color tone that pops in bouquets and is especially beautiful with orange! There's no other zinnia quite like it; grow to 32 to 36 inches (80 to 90 cm) tall with 3- to 5-inch (7.5 to 13 cm) blooms.

'Zowie!™ Yellow Flame' is perfect for fall bouquets. It features rows of brilliant yellow-tipped orange petals with a large magenta cone center. The blooms change color as they mature, and the cone appears to get smaller each day as more petals grow to fill in around it. It's a real showstopper and butterflies adore it; grows 28 to 32 inches (70 to 80 cm) tall with 2- to 3-inch (5 to 7.5 cm) blooms.

The first warm-season tender annual beds of the season with zinnias and marigolds. All beds are covered in biodegradable film with the black side up and flower support netting is installed.

Resources

Irrigation Supplies & Tutorials

- **Berry Hill Irrigation:** www.berryhillirrigation.com

- **DripWorks:** www.dripworks.com

Plug & Plants

- **Ball Seed,** plug supplier for growers: http://ballseed.com/cutflowers/

- **Burpee,** for plants for home gardeners including lisianthus: www.burpee.com

- **Farmer Bailey,** plug supplier for growers: https://farmerbailey.com

- **Germania Seed,** plug supplier for growers: www.germaniaseed.com

Seeds

- **Ardelia Farm** (sweet pea seeds), for home gardeners and growers: www.ardeliafarm.com

- **Ball Seed,** seed supplier for growers: http://ballseed.com/cutflowers/

- **Germania Seed,** seed supplier for growers: www.germaniaseed.com

- **Johnny's Selected Seeds,** supplies home gardeners and growers: www.johnnyseeds.com

- **The Gardener's Workshop,** supplies home gardeners and growers: www.TheGardenersWorkshop.com

- **Floret,** supplies home gardeners and growers: www.floretflowers.com

- **Harris Seeds,** supplies home gardeners and growers: www.harrisseeds.com

Seed Starting Equipment, Garden & Cut-Flower Supplies

- **Johnny's Selected Seeds,** supplies home gardeners and growers: www.johnnyseeds.com

- **The Gardener's Workshop,** supplies home gardeners and growers: www.TheGardenersWorkshop.com

About the Author

Lisa is an author, leader in the cut-flower industry, accomplished speaker, online teacher, and the owner of TheGardenersWorkshop.com. What began in 1998 as a small urban cut-flower farm producing for local markets has grown into so much more. Pursuing her passion to help others grow flowers has grown her business into an educational platform for home gardeners and budding to seasoned flower farmers. Her flagship online course, Flower Farming School Online, has reached thousands of students worldwide, empowering them to grow and sell flowers profitably.

Connect with Lisa at TheGardenersWorkshop.com to find her videos, blog, podcasts, online courses, and live events. Visit her online garden shop that stocks her autographed books and the same tools, seeds, and supplies she uses in her gardens.

Acknowledgments

My love of gardening, farming, and teaching has been enriched by those that want to learn more about growing cut flowers. The interest expressed has led me to teach, share, and show the way for many like I never knew I could. This encourages me daily, thank you!

Never would I have dreamed a decade ago that I would become a published author. Yet, here we are, in book number three. As one with dyslexia who struggled to read and write for the first half of my life, nothing seemed farther from my reach than authoring a book. Through the guidance and support of my personal editor, Susan Yoder Ackerman, and others, I was led to get my words onto these pages. For this opportunity I am forever grateful. Even though the writer is the most visible, it takes many hands to make a book happen, some I must mention by name.

The entire team at The Gardener's Workshop kept our multifaceted business running smoothly in my absence. I would never have had the courage to tackle this book project without their support. This team of gardeners, flower farmers, and flower lovers filled in seamlessly to cover all the bases, and I thank each one of you!

To TGW team member and my co-author, Jessi Graven, thank you! It was as though we went together like bread and butter in this book.

Jessi's flower-farming experiences, attention to detail, and writing skills fit this project perfectly. I am so grateful for the input, research, and contributions you provided.

Bob Scharmerhorn's photographs bring the words on these pages to life to entice readers. I appreciate his beautiful images, skill, and his easy-going manner that makes working with him a pleasure. This is our second book together and his attention to detail and to my endless list of photos to take is priceless to me. Thank you, Bob!

I appreciate that Jessica Walliser, editorial director at Cool Springs Press, saw my vision and took a gamble on me. The art and editorial staff at Quarto crafted the images and words that brought this beautiful book to life. Thank you!

The one constant in my flower farming and business life has been my sister, Suzanne Mason Frye. She always comes through to do whatever is needed, and in this book, she became the stand-in photographer. I literally could not have done it without her. Thank you, sister.

Perhaps the one that makes all I do possible is my best friend and husband, Stevie. From business talk over dinner to helping prepare meals and doing laundry, I couldn't do any of this without you babe!

Index